电视新闻主播话语中的立场与评价

STANCE AND APPRAISAL IN TELEVISION NEWS PRESENTATION

朱红强 著

《暨南外语博士文库》

主编/宫 齐

副主编/程 倩 廖开洪 蒲若茜 王 琢

世界图书出版公司
广州·上海·西安·北京

图书在版编目（CIP）数据

电视新闻主播话语中的立场与评价：英文/朱红强著. —广州：世界图书出版广东有限公司，2018.12
ISBN 978-7-5192-5483-4

Ⅰ. ①电… Ⅱ. ①朱… Ⅲ. ①电视新闻－新闻语言－研究—英文Ⅳ. ①G220

中国版本图书馆 CIP 数据核字（2018）第 284379 号

书　　名 电视新闻主播话语中的立场与评价
DIANSHI XINWEN ZHUBO HUAYU ZHONG DE LICHANG YU PINGJIA
著　　者 朱红强
责任编辑 程　静
装帧设计 苏　婷
责任技编 刘上锦
出版发行 世界图书出版广东有限公司
地　　址 广州市新港西路大江冲 25 号
邮　　编 510300
电　　话 020-84451969　84453623　84184026　84459579
网　　址 http://www.gdst.com.cn
邮　　箱 wpc_gdst@163.com
经　　销 各地新华书店
印　　刷 广州市迪桦彩印有限公司
开　　本 787 mm × 1 092 mm　1/16
印　　张 10
字　　数 300 千字
版　　次 2018 年 12 月第 1 版　2018 年 12 月第 1 次印刷
国际书号 ISBN 978-7-5192-5483-4
定　　价 38.00 元

咨询、投稿：020－84451258　gdstchj@126.com

本书为广东省哲学社会科学“十三五”规划2018年度项目“外语学科专项”项目的部分研究成果。项目名称：“内涵式”教育模式下英语专业教师身份构建的话语研究（立项编号：GD18WZX32）。

总 序

素有“华侨最高学府”之称的暨南大学创办于 1906 年,是我国第一所由政府创办的华侨高等学府,是国务院侨办、教育部、广东省共建的“211 工程”重点综合性大学,也是目前在全国招收港澳台和海外华人华侨学生最多的高校。“暨南”二字出自《尚书 · 禹贡》篇:“东渐于海,西被于流沙,朔南暨,声教讫于四海。”意即面向南洋,将中华文化远播至五洲四海。

暨南大学的前身是 1906 年清政府创立于南京的暨南学堂。1927 年迁至上海,更名为国立暨南大学。抗日战争期间,迁址福建建阳。1946 年迁回上海,三年后合并于复旦大学、交通大学等高校。中华人民共和国成立后,暨南大学于 1958 年在广州重建,“文革”期间曾一度停办,1978 年复办。1996 年 6 月,暨南大学成为全国面向 21 世纪重点建设的大学。学校恪守“忠信笃敬”之校训,积极贯彻“面向海外,面向港澳台”的办学方针,建校迄今共培养了来自世界五大洲 160 多个国家和港澳台地区的各类人才近 30 余万人。

暨南大学外国语学院的前身是创办于1927年的外国语言文学系，历史上曾有许多著名专家、学者在该系任教，如叶公超、梁实秋、钱钟书、许国璋教授等。1978年复办后，外语系在曾昭科、翁显良两位教授的主持下，教学与科研成绩斐然，1981年外国语言文学系获国家第一批硕士学位授予权，成为暨南大学最早拥有硕士授予权的单位之一。当时的英语语言文学硕士点以文学为主、专长翻译，翁显良、曾昭科、张鸾铃、谭时霖、黄均、黄锡祥教授等一大批优秀学者先后担任硕士研究生导师，他们治学严谨，成绩卓著，为我们今天的发展奠定了坚实的基础。

如今，外国语学院已拥有专任教师133人，其中教授10人，副教授46人，讲师69人。教授中有博士生导师3人，硕士生导师39人。学院教师中获博士学位者近50人，在读博士近20人。现有英语系、商务英语系、日语系、法语系和大学英语教学部等5个教学单位；有英美文学研究所、应用语言学研究所、跨文化及翻译研究所、日本语言文化研究所及外语教学研究所等5个研究机构。学院现有外国语言文学硕士学位一级学科授权点一个，有英语语言文学、外国语言学及应用语言学、日语语言文学3个二级学科，以及翻译专业硕士（MTI）学位授权点。英语语言文学方向主要为华裔美国文学研究、英美女性文学和后现代文学研究；外国语言学及应用语言学方向以理论语言学、功能语言学和音系学为研究特色；日语语言文学方向侧重现当代日本文学、日中比较文学、日语语言及文化研究；翻译方向从语言学、文学和文化等多个层面探讨翻译理论与实践，突出翻译的实践性。研究生导师大多数具有海外大学或学术机构从事教学、科研、进修的经历。目前，学院教师主持国家社科基金项目9项，教育部、广东省社科规划项目数十项。

《暨南外语博士文库》系列丛书（以下简称《文库》系列丛书）的编纂，主要基于以下目的：首先，是对近十几年来暨南大学外语学科获得博士学位教师研究成果的梳理和总结；其次，为学院的中、青年外语骨干教师搭建展示团队科研成果的平台，以显示学科发展的集群效应；第三，旨在激励更多的暨南外语学人（特别是青年学子）不断进取，勇攀教学、科研的新高峰，再创新辉煌。《文库》系列丛书主要收录了2000年以后我校外语学科博士学位获得者尚未正式出版的博士论文，这些论文均经本人反复修改和校对，再经相关博士生导师的认真审阅和作者本人最终修改后方提交出版社排版付梓。该套丛书涵盖了语言学、外国文学、文化、翻译及其他相关领域，所涉及的语种包括汉语、英语、日语、法语和西班牙语等。《文库》系列丛书的第一辑10部现已出全，第二辑10部正在陆续修改、校对和编排中。

《文库》系列丛书是新一代暨南外语学人孜孜不倦，努力拼搏和进取所取得的研究硕果，是他们宁静致远，潜心治学的象征。这些成果代表了暨南外语学科的进步与发展，预示着我们的希望和未来，也是我们献给暨南大学110周年校庆和外国语学院建院90周年华诞的一份丰厚礼物。

《文库》系列丛书的出版分别得到了广东省优势重点学科基金、学校重点学科建设项目和广东省高水平大学建设基金的支持，世界图书出版广东有限公司的编辑在丛书的编辑、审校、设计等方面亦付出了大量心血，在此我们一并表示衷心感谢！

编　者

2016年11月16日

Contents

List of Tables and Figures

Chapter 1　Introduction: Objectives of Study

1.1　Introduction

Despite the increasing impact of digital communication, television remains a high-profile medium, a widely established means of communication, which exerts a huge influence over people's social lives. According to the yearly report of Customer Service Management in China, television had an audience of 1.28 billion in China in 2013, including 1.27 billion in mainland China and 6.40 million in Hong Kong. In the latest annual report of the Chinese Social Science Academy, television and print newspapers as traditional media were still considered the most credible media for the Chinese people, with trust indices of 81.1% and 70.3%, respectively (Liu, 2013). By comparison, the British Broadcasting Corporation (BBC), a public service broadcaster, is a highly trusted television platform, which gained 83.1% audience appreciation in 2012 – 2013. In addition, the BBC retained a very strong position with audiences, according to the 2012 –

2013 BBC annual report[①], with 86% of the population in Britain watching BBC television every week.

Television news is a significant component for television output and television news takes a variety of forms ranging from 24-hour rolling news to regular bulletin news. In whatever form, news readers or news presenters, or news casters reading news on television is the stable feature. Within television news, for the purpose of this study, news presentation is the delivery of news more often by someone who reads it directly for the audience. As animators of the discourse, news readers, news presenters, or news casters adopt an institutional voice, in which the discourse is more or less devoid of personal expression in the service of the journalistic goals of balance, impartiality or objectivity.

However, achieving the goal of objectivity to which journalists aspire is to some degree an illusion, a point argued widely in the literature (see Bednarek, 2006a; Fairclough, 1988; Fowler, 1991; Hartley, 1982; White, 1997, 2000, 2006). On the other hand, television news presentations are commonly authored by someone (typically an editorial team) for the television audience; therefore, they are rarely immune from the

① BBC annual report and account 2012/13. Part 2. The BBC Executive's Review and Assessment. http://downloads.bbc.co.uk/annualreport/pdf/2012-13/bbc-bbcexecutive-annualreport-review-and-assessment-2012-13.pdf expression of attitudes, and opinions. Indeed, just as White (2006) claims regarding news reports in the press, it might be argued that TV news presentation reflects the rhetoric of 'a value-laden, ideologically determined discourse with a clear potential to influence the media audience's assumptions and beliefs about the way the world is and the way it ought to be' (p. 37).

It is the contention of this study that some degree of personal stance -influenced by different factors (e. g., social, economic, corporate)-will inevitably be reflected in the discourse of news presentation. From the perspective of the linguist, therefore, it is important to spell out the factors, such as rhetorical devices or other linguistic mechanisms, which underpin the particular realisations of stance which we encounter. Using this approach, we can begin to understand how stance is institutionalized in a cultural context and in what ways the operation of stance may vary across contexts (e. g., situations or cultures).

1.2 Purpose and Background of the Study

My argument begins, therefore, with the premise that TV news discourse, particularly news presentation, cannot be devoid of attitude and stance. The question, then, arises: in what ways does the discourse of television news presentation adopt different kinds of stance. The purpose of the study, therefore, is to explore how different linguistic realisations of stance may reflect different institutional positions, through comparing the different linguistic resources and selections across two culturally distinct broadcasters, Chinese Central Television (CCTV) and the BBC.

In this sense the thesis explores the paradox whereby the inevitable operation of linguistic stance undermines the common claims of objectivity, impartiality and balance. As shown in the linguistic literature, and especially in the classic works of critical tradition (Fairclough, 1995; Fowler, 1991; van Dijk, 1988a; van Leeuwen, 1987) the signs of authorial stance and subjectivity can be detected in terms of the different linguistic selections adopted in the news. Indeed, their analyses revealed how sets of ideational or representational choices can serve to naturalize particular points of views and legitimize different kinds of ideological positioning. The shared project underlying their approach was the disclosure of the power relationships and biased representations hidden behind news discourse. However, these classic studies all focused on linguistic modes of representation in the press with little or no attention to stance. In order to address this gap, I apply linguistic analysis of the authorial stance with the broadcast news.

The other reason for studying stance in the discourse of television news presentation from a linguistic perspective was that linguists have long been interested in the language of print journalism. However, except for some isolated papers (Pounds, 2012) and chapters in a book (Haarman & Lombardo, 2009), there have been far fewer studies of stance in the discourse of broadcast news, compared with studies of print news (Allan, 1998; Bednarek, 2006a; Fairclough, 1989, 1992, 1995; Iedema, Feez & White, 1994; Marín-Arrese et al., 2004; Martin & White, 2005; O'Keeffe & Breen, 2007; Pounds, 2010; van Dijk, 1988a, 1988b; White, 1998). And yet, news broadcasts on television draw upon a set of verbal practices different from those of print news (Montgomery, 2007). The rhetorical or ideological functions of the language employed by broadcasters vary from those used by print journalists and consequently may influence audiences to position themselves attitudinally (positively or negatively) to the events depicted in ways different from print news. This thesis therefore sets out to capture how rhetorical functions-especially as realized in stance-are patterned in the institutional discourses of television not just on one broadcaster but how these patterns may vary across culturally distinct broadcasters.

1.3 Comparative Dimension of Stance in Television News Presentation

This comparative study of institutional stance was based on the assumption that stance is invariably encoded at some level linguistically and will be more or less differently conveyed to audiences due to differences in verbal practices.

The comparative dimension adopted in this dissertation was the essential feature of its methodology, which was supported by research on news frames or information processing schemata (Entman, 1991). The different ways of conceptualizing the same events and framing them within a field of meaning choices may result in variations of stance provided by the different news broadcasters. As Entman (1991) suggested,

> Frames reside in the specific properties of news narrative that encourage those perceiving and thinking about events to develop particular understandings of them. News frames are constructed from and embodies in the keywords, metaphors, concepts, symbols, and visual images emphasized in a news narratives...Frames can be detected by probing for a particular words and visual images that consistently appear in a narrative and convey thematically consonant meanings

> across media and time... Through repetition, placement, and reinforcing associations with each other, the words and images that comprise the frame render one basic interpretation more readily discernible, comprehensible, and memorable than others. (p. 7)

> Entman (1991) also pointed out that the importance of comparative dimension is to reveal the critical textual choices that framed the story but would otherwise remain submerged in an undifferentiated text. Unless narratives are compared, frames are difficult to detect fully and reliably, because many of the framing devices can appear as 'natural', unremarkable choices or words or images. (p. 6)

For the purposes of comparison, therefore, two main established broadcasters, CCTV and BBC, were chosen. CCTV and BBC are two socioculturally distinct news institutions: CCTV is a state-owned television station in China that serves as both a mouthpiece for the Communist Party of China and as a platform to the outside to profile the party's image and publicize its ideology; the BBC is an international public service broadcaster in Britain funded principally by public levy through a license fee. The sociocultural differences reflected or refracted through their journalistic practices and television news presentations could thus be assumed to be important arenas through which to discern the differences between their institutional voices. However, as journalistic institutions, both the CCTV and the BBC claim to abide by some common principles of professional ethics (e. g., The Professional Ethics of Chinese Journalism, Item 3; see Appendix 1 and *British Broadcasting Corporation [BBC] Editorial Guideline*①), including impartiality, objectivity, fairness and truthfulness. This paradox, as mentioned previously, served as the main motivation for conducting a comparative study of the CCTV and the BBC to determine whether variations exist in stance between the news presentation of either broadcaster and, if such variations do exist, on what dimensions they operate.

The news delivered by the news presenter, understood to be the main carrier of institutional voice, is always subject to selection and editorial processes conducted prior to broadcasts. These processes involve journalistic coding, such as the choice of words and grammatical and rhetorical devices and the organization of the message. As professional as journalists may be, ensuring the news is devoid of opinion is difficult. Therefore, journalists must distil personal knowledge, interpretation, and **judgement** in deciding what lexical items or

① BBC editorial guidelines. http://www.bbc.co.uk/editorialguidelines/guidelines/

grammatical devices to employ in composing a news story. For example, one could argue that the overt wording in the following two phrases is indicative of opposing stances: 'Tibetan protesters' versus 'Tibetan separatists'. Variations in the references to the disputed islands between China and Japan may also indicate variations in stance in news coverage. The use of 'Senkaku/Diaoyu' islands appeared in the BBC news, representing a neutral stance; the exclusive use of 'Diaoyu islands' in the CCTV news represented China's territorial claim.[①] Thus, differences in stance are clearly and differently represented in the choice of phrases; and such differences may coincide with or reflect different political contexts and ideological biases.

When an event is encoded and represented by different institutions, the stance adopted in the news presentations is likely to vary. To illustrate this, Table 1 shows a comparison of the same event presented by the BBC and the CCTV. As seen in the two texts, each institution verbalized the event somewhat differently. The textual choices showed variations of attitude toward the event, with the alternative point of view reflected through the

① The Diaoyu/Senkaku islands are a group of islands located in the East Sea of China. 'Diaoyu islands' is Chinese pinyin for 'fishing islands', which are also known as the Senkaku Islands in Japanese. Diaoyu islands/Senkaku islands are disputed on the sovereignty over the territory between P. R. China and Japan. P. R. China claims them as territorial ownership for the discovery of these islands in the 14th century; and Japan claims their ownership since the transfer of administrative controls in 1971 from the United States.

differing representations of ‘evaluated entities’ (Thetela, 1997, p. 103) or attitudinal ‘target’ (White, 2004, p. 233) in the reporter’s voice.

Table 1 Comparison of Verbal Representations of the Same News Event: The Killing of an Afghan Civilian by a U. S. Soldier

Institution/ broadcast date	Scenes of the news reports (screenshots)	News presenter’s discourse
British Broadcasting Corporation: 03/12/2012	 	The Afghan president Hamid Karzai has condemned the killings of 16 civilians by a rogue American soldier as unforgivable. The victims, nine of whom are children, were shot dead early on Sunday morning in their homes in Kandahar province. President Obama telephoned Mr Karzai to express his shock and to offer his condolences. He said he was deeply saddened. Quentin Sommerville sent this report from Afghan capital and I should warn you: this contains some distressing images.
Chinese Central Television: 03/12/2012	 	A U. S. soldier is being held after killing at least sixteen Afghan civilians in a shooting rampage in Kandahar province. NATO officials have apologized for Sunday’s attack, saying they’ll investigate the incident. The killings are likely to further strain relations between U. S. forces and their Afghan hosts with Afghan President Hamid Karzai branding the incident as ‘intentional murders’.

Generally, both texts depicted the event as a tragic accident, adopting a negative stance towards it by reporting the participants' reactions or treatments to this event (e. g., BBC text: 'President Hamid Karzai condemned the killings'; 'President Obama was saddened and shocked'; CCTV text: 'NATO officials apologized for Sunday's attack', 'A U. S. soldier is held after his killing'). Furthermore, Afghan president Hamid Karzai was described as unhappy with, or even angry at, this accident, because he 'condemned' the act of killing (BBC text) and brands it as 'intentional murder' (CCTV text). The U. S. President 'Obama' was represented as 'saddened' and seemed very sympathetic to the victims in the BBC text. The differences of choice of words in the two texts may lead to variations in the attitude projected to the participants to some extent. Even, the use of a single modifier indicated one extra assessment in one news text in comparison with the other. For example, 'an American soldier' was modified with the word 'rogue' in the BBC text, a word that added more negative overtones to 'the single soldier' than in the CCTV text. No direct equivalence between the stances adopted by the reported participants and their news reporting stances exists; but when journalists approach an event, they must make decisions regarding which descriptive details to note, which sources to approach, and what to include in their reports. For journalists, selection of the materials is not an objective process. For example, the simple act of choosing words is an active and personal decision that requires journalists to interpret the information they obtain and the meaning of the words. Moreover, this act is not a comprehensive act of reporting because the audience receives only a partial understanding of the reality. This was shown in the unequal presence of the participants in the two reports: one of the reported participants, American president Obama, is present in the BBC text but absent in the CCTV text. Similarly, 'NATO officials' are reported in the CCTV text but not in the BBC text. The presence or absence of some participant (s) in news reports revealed that news materials are necessarily subject to a process of journalistic construction.

For journalists, quoting participants' utterances has been a routine procedure and a strategic ritual of objectivity (Tuchman, 1972), implying that journalists usually attribute interpretation of issues or events to the participants to support the journalists' 'truth-claims' to achieve objectivity. As shown in the example, the attitudes provided in the news concerning the accountability of the killing incident shifted from one participant to another due to the selection of the attributed voice. In the BBC text, the voice of President Obama's utterance was quoted (i. e., 'He said he was deeply saddened'); the phrase 'deeply saddened' merely coloured the emotional response of the U. S. government that is administered by President Obama. The CCTV text quoted a voice not from the U. S. government but from NATO (i. e., 'NATO officials have apologized for Sunday's attack, saying they'll investigate the incident'). The quoted voice of NATO indicated the intergovernmental mediation involved in this incident. Thus, the U. S. soldier's killing became an international concern through the highlighting of the role of NATO as the party responsible for investigating the 'illegal action'. In either text, however, the missing voice (i. e., either the U. S. government or NATO) could give rise to positioning the audience to have no evaluative attitude toward the absent source. Thus, evaluation of the 'targets' or 'entities' in reported speech might reflect journalistic subjectivity, including preferences, biases, or the directness of evaluation.

The comparative observation of this single case between CCTV and BBC reveals the different linguistic elements or rhetorical devices employed and the different purposes of the broadcasters. Variations of language in use not only shape the news but also depict the world in different ways. Meanings expressed through the use of words, phrases, rhetorical devices, and linguistic mechanisms position audiences in relation to the reported entities and events. Therefore, a systematic comparative study between the CCTV and the BBC should show linguistic variations in reporting the same events across cultures, revealing the extent to which and by what linguistic means the CCTV news maps the world differently than the BBC news. In other words, such a study should show how differently events are mediated through the use of lexis and grammar across the institutional-cultural contexts thereby undermining any simple notion of ' facticity' and objectivity.

1.4 The Objectives and Research Questions

This dissertation was based on a cross-cultural study to examine how stance operates in two socially distinct discourse environments, namely, CCTV and BBC. The objectives of this study were

- specifying and delineating the types of stance featured in the discourse of television news presentation;
- investigating how stance operates in television news presentation from the two channels;
- comparing stance realisation in the discourse of television news presentation across cultures; and
- exploring the possible factors that affect stance

realisation and variation in the overall discourse practice.

Based on those objectives, the following four research questions served to guide this study:

RQ1: Through what linguistic mechanisms or rhetorical devices does stance operate in the discourse of television news presentation (e. g., the CCTV news and the BBC news)?

RQ2: Are there consistent patterns or variations in the realisation of stance in the CCTV and the BBC television news presentations?

RQ3: If variation in the realisation of stance between the CCTV and the BBC exists, on what dimensions does each variation occur?

RQ4: What are the possible factors to interpret variation in the realisation of stance between and within the CCTV and the BBC?

1.5 Outline of the Dissertation

The dissertation consists of three main parts and contains eihgt chapters. Part 1, which consists of chapters 1 – 3, is a presentation of the research background and contextualisation of the present dissertation within the domain of discourse analysis. Chapter 1 contains an introduction to the notions of stance and television news presentation and a rationale for the research that is focused on stance realisation in the discourse of television news presentation. Chapter 2 contains a literature review on television news presentation, stance, and its related notions. Chapter 3 consists of a recapitulation of appraisal theory as the conceptual framework for the dissertation, along with White's (2006) extended framework as the tool used in analysis. This chapter also introduces the discourse of television news presentation collected as data, including descriptions of the data collection and coding used in this study.

Part 2, which consists of chapters 4 – 7, is concerned with analysis of the four cases examined in this study. Each chapter focuses on a specific case so as to explore how stance operates in the discourse of television news presentation in both the CCTV and BBC contexts. The four cases were analysed in terms of the variables advanced in White's framework. In general, these variables included the three aspects of stance: attitude, attribution, and agency and affectedness. The themes of the four cases ranged from warfare, and socioeconomic disruptions to natural disasters. The choice of themes was expected to build a comprehensive picture of stance variations within and between individual institutional discourses.

Part 3 consists of chapter 8, the conclusion of the dissertation. This chapter is a summary of the patterns of stance variation in the overall representation of each institution. The chapter also contains a discussion of the findings in the case studies and elaboration concerning the representation of stance variations across events and broadcasters. A discussion of the limitations and further implications of this research has also been included.

Chapter 2 Literature Review: Stance and Television News Presentation

2.1 Introduction

This thesis aims to explore the cross-cultural variations of attitude, value or position adopted in the discourse of television news presentation by examining stance. In any social encounter, speakers or writers not only present propositions about things, facts, events, and happenings but also express viewpoints, attitudes, and emotions relative to these propositional contents, as well as taking up a position in relation to their addressees. In a general sense, stance may be understood as the expression by a speaker of a particular attitude to the proposition being uttered or to the audience to whom the utterance is addressed.

This chapter consists of two sections: (a) a review of the literature on stance and (b) a review of the literature on television news presentation. The first section begins with the relevance of stance studies to appraisal theory applied as a methodology to the linguistic realisation of stance in news discourse. The second section includes a proposed definition of television news presentation, a review of stance studies of television news presentation, and the journalistic voice of television news presentation.

2.2 Stance and Appraisal Theory

Within linguistics, Biber and Finegan (1988) originally adopted the term *stance* to mean the 'overt expression of an author's or speaker's attitudes, feelings, judgements, or commitments concerning the message' (p. 1). Shortly afterwards, they defined stance as 'the lexical and grammatical expression of attitudes, feelings, judgements, or commitment concerning the propositional content of a message' (Biber & Finegan, 1989, p. 93). Biber and Finegan's initial ideas of stance are only broadly concerned with the linguistic expression of speaker's attitude to the message. Later, they suggest that 'stance can be expressed to a differing extent through grammatical devices, value-laden word choice and paralinguistic devices' (Biber et al. p. 966). Biber et. al. (1999) use the term to deal with quite specific devices that linguistically and paralinguistically realise stance or attitudes of speakers to the proposition. Moreover, stance can be distinguished into different types. For instance, Conrad and Biber (2000) conducted a statistical study of the adverbial marking of stance in a corpus across registers, identifying three kinds of meanings associated with the speaker's or writer's attitude or stance towards what the person was saying: (a) epistemic stance (relating to the certainty the speaker or writer holds to the source of the message); (b) attitudinal stance (indicating feelings or judgements about what is said or written); and (c) style stance (associated with how the message is said or written).

In social interaction, stance involves not only projection of viewpoints and expression of attitude to the propositions but also construction of interpersonal relationships. Later work proposed that stance should not be restricted only to attribute value/attitude to propositions but should also encompass qualities of relationship between interactants. Johnstone (2009), for example, stated that 'stance is generally understood to have to do with the methods, linguistic and other, by which interactants create and signal relationship with the propositions they utter and with the people they interact with' (p. 31). One should note therefore, especially in the light of Johnstone's words, that stance seems to deal with two kinds of relationships: (a) the speaker's relationship with the propositions uttered and (b) the speaker's relationship with the addressee. Going beyond Johnstone's static approach to stance, Du Bois's approach to stance considers stance as a social act in a more dynamically social interaction. His 'stance triangle' (2007) suggested that one could treat stance as a public act, which is performed by a social actor (stance-taker) through communicative means (linguistic, paralinguistic, etc.) in social encounters to achieve three goals simultaneously: 'evaluate objects, position subjects (themselves and others), and align with other subjects, with respect to any salient dimension of the sociocultural field' (Du Bois, 2007, p. 163). In other words, with this 'triangle', Du Bois (2007) moved beyond Johnstone's (2009) approach in noting that stance positions the speaker as well as the audience (the hearers).

As well as different definitions of stance, different researchers adopt different approaches to identifying and analyzing 'stance markers'. Variations of stance can be identified through different uses of linguistic resources and language mechanisms. For example, Biber and Finegan (1989) analysed adverbials in English as stance markers by means of corpus-based investigation, classifying them into six semantic categories: 'honestly adverbials', 'generally adverbials', 'surely adverbials', 'actually adverbials', 'maybe adverbials', and 'amazingly adverbials'. They also interpreted the discourse functions of these stance markers in texts. In addition, stance markers are not only found in written texts to organize discourses and express points of view but they can also be identified as working in conversational encounters. Conrad and Biber (2000) conducted a statistical study of the adverbial marking of stance in a corpus across registers (conversations, academic writing and news reportage), identifying three kinds of meanings associated with the speaker's or writer's attitude or stance towards what the person was saying: (a) epistemic stance, (b) attitudinal stance, and (c) style stance. For example, they pointed to the role of grammatical adverbials 'to express meanings associated with the speaker or writer's attitude to what he or she is saying' (p. 56). Along with their study, which is primarily focused on stance realization by 'grammatical' elements, Kärkkäinen (2006), for instance, discussed *I think* as an epistemic stance marker in conversation and Du Bois (2004) examined the stance markers *too* and *either* to build alignment between a current stance and a prior one. Indeed, such markers as *I think* in conversations, which have been explored as 'discourse markers' in sociolinguistics (Schiffrin, 1986; Swan, 2005), are identified as indicating a speaker's attitude towards what is being said and towards the other participants. In addition, other linguistic devices may well mark stances of speakers or manage interpersonal relationships between the speaker and the hearer, especially in a sequence of conversation. For example, Clift (2006) discussed reported speech, one of a variety of linguistic mechanisms with which speakers lay claim to epistemic priority vis-a-vis recipients, in the sequential context of interaction.

As a theoretical concept in the literature, authors have explored aspects of stance in several ways: as 'evaluation' (Thompson & Hunston, 2000; Hunston, 2000; Bednarek, 2006a), as 'meta-discourse' (Hyland, 2005a), and as 'appraisal' (Martin, 2000; Martin & White, 2005). Evaluation in the approach of Thompson & Hunston (Thompson & Hunston, 2000) is the 'broad cover term for expression of the speaker or writer's attitude or stance towards, viewpoint on, or feelings about the entities or propositions that he or she is talking about' (p. 5). However, unlike Biber and Finegan's work (1989) on stance, who provided a list of 'stance markers' comprising lexical items from particular word class and other categories, Thompson and Hunston (2000) only suggest that the role of evaluation is important in discourse and works on different planes of discourse, but they were unable to map out a picture of linguistic devices or resources to systematically capture the expression of the speaker or writer's stance or attitude.

Stance as a term has also been used by Hyland (2005a) when referring to meta-discourse as ‘aspects of a text which explicitly organize a discourse or a writer’s stance towards either its contents or the reader’ (p. 14). Hyland (2005b) has also suggested that stance expresses ‘a textual “voice” or community recognized personality’ and involves attitudinal features that reflect the ways ‘writers present themselves and convey their judgements, opinions and commitments’ (p. 176). Hence, stance ‘positions’ writers and enables them to ‘stamp their personal authority onto their arguments or step back and disguise their involvement’ (p. 176). Hyland (2005a), indeed, proposed a set of meta-discursive resources (i. e., interactive resources and interactional resources) that are thought to organize propositional information and involve readers in various ways. His model of meta-discourse was applied to analyse writers’ authorial stances provided in academic discourse (Hyland, 2005a, 2006, 2007).

As suggested above, stance deals with two relationships within the writer/speaker’s attitude. One is the relationship between the propositions of an utterance and the utterer (i. e., speakers’/writers’ attitudes to the propositions they utter). The other is the relationship between the utterer and the addressee (i. e., how speakers/writers position and evaluate addressees through language).

However, neither Biber's nor Hyland's approach to stance is able to thoroughly delineate the attitude of speakers to the proposition as well as taking up a position to their addressee. Both Biber and Hyland offered a catalogue of linguistic categories to project subjectivity of speakers and writers, but the assignment of linguistic categories in either model is not comprehensively developed. Hyland's model, for instance, suggests that ' meta-discourse' expresses interpersonal relationship between writer and reader but this model neglects the attitudes signposted in the propositional contents of utterance. In addition, categories of stance markers for Biber and his colleagues are based on grammatical forms in discourse instead of discourse semantics. Except adverbial marking of stance, their works do not deal even with the lexical semantics of attitude in textual message, nor do they deal with the interactive positioning taken up by the speakers or writers to their addressees. Therefore, the above approaches to stance offer only a partial analytic framework to the stance expressed by the speakers or writers. Appraisal theory seems to be a more advantageous model in dealing with the attitudes of the speakers and writers in relation to the propositions and to their positioning of their addressees, because appraisal theory builds a more comprehensive system to frame the types of attitudinal subjectivity expressed in the locutions and the sorts of inter-subjective stances taken up by the speakers and writers to their addressees.

Rooted within systemic function linguistics (SFL) and treated as part of the interpersonal function of language expressed in texts, appraisal theory provides a set of semantic resources as a means through which speakers/writers not only express their feelings and assume a stance but also 'engage with socially-determined value positions and thereby align or dis-align themselves with the social subjects who hold to these positions' (White, 2011, p. 14). In appraisal theory, semantic resources and subjectivity are classified into three systems: attitude, engagement, and graduation. Attitude concerns the resources for expressing feelings, 'including emotional reactions, judgements of behaviour and evaluation of things' (Martin & White, 2005, p. 35). Engagement involves 'sourcing attitudes and the play of voices around opinions in discourse' (Martin & White, 2005, p. 35). Graduation deals with 'grading phenomena whereby feelings are amplified and categories blurred' (Martin & White, 2005, p. 35). The systems of discourse semantics modelled by appraisal theory involve the inscribed and invoked realisations of attitudinal stance and the intersubjective positioning in discourse. As we shall see below, appraisal theory would seem to offer a comprehensive framework by which to model and analyse the realisation of stance provided by television news presentation.

For example, after the Boston Marathon Bombing on 16 April 2013, the BBC presented one of its news items in this way: ' British Prime Minister David Cameron released a statement saying the scenes from Boston are *shocking*. That's a quote from him. "*My thoughts*," he says, "*are with all those who have been affected*" ' (BBC World News, 16 – 04 – 2013). The lexis ' shocking' in *Collins Cobuild Advanced British English Dictionary* (2007) is defined as ' *you can say that something is shocking if you think that it is bad* (*or morally wrong*)' (p. 1205) and apparently its semantics expresses the speaker's negative feeling toward the Boston Bombing and this is an explicit appraisal of the event, which encodes the speaker's negative judgement of the act of bombing. Furthermore, this negative appraisal is followed up with the presenter's quote of Prime Minister David Cameron ' my thoughts are with all those who have been affected' and this utterance quoted is semantically neutral but carries no explicit evaluation of people or things. However, appraisal theory tends to regard the utterance of Prime Minister David Cameron within its context as an attitude ' invoked' -a negative affect and this invoked affect helps to understand the speaker's feeling, i. e., Prime Minister David Cameron is sympathetic about the victims who are affected from the Boston Bombing.

Thus, appraisal theory not only is able to identify the explicit and implicit realization of attitude in news texts but also works to picture the dimensions of attitude.

Moreover, in news discourse, the attributions of statement to external sources can be understood as a strategic ritual of 'objectivity' (Tuchman, 1972). This feature corresponds with appraisal resource 'attribute' within the system 'engagement' modelled in appraisal theory. In this case, the utterance of British Prime Minister David Cameron was quoted by BBC journalists. Attribution was fulfilled with the reporting words 'statement' and 'say', but the reporting words presented the audience with attributed materials (e. g., 'the scenes from Boston are shocking' and 'my thoughts are with all those who have been affected') as warrantable and highly credible because the assessment of high credibility was invoked by the high social status of the source, British Prime Minister David Cameron.

Overall, stance in this case worked on both levels. One was the linguistic realisation of subjective attitudes in the propositions; the other was oriented to intersubjective positioning of stance by means of rhetorical strategies such as attribution. Indeed, stance remains a dynamic and abstract process; the semantic load of stance naturally varies from one news item to another. In searching for a methodological benchmark to examine how stance operates in the discourse of television news presentation, appraisal theory seems to offer a relatively comprehensive framework by which to compare one institutional stance with another.

Using appraisal theory, one can map the meaning resources in language within the interpersonal strand in terms of three areas of attitude, engagement, and graduation. Taking each in turn, the aim of attitude is to identify the evaluative lexis or the tokens used by the writer/speaker to encode entities in the world. **Attitude** is realised in terms of three subcategories or regions: **affect**, **judgement**, and **appreciation**. The systems of engagement and graduation are grounded in the dialogism of utterance; their aim is to cover intersubjective positioning concerning the message, which projects the relationship between the utterer and the addressee. As White (2003) contends, the linguistic resources of intersubjective positioning can be brought together in appraisal theory on the ground of discourse semantics because 'they all provide the means for speakers/writers to take a stance towards the various points-of-view or social positionings being referenced by the text and thereby to position themselves with respect to the other social subjects who hold those positions' (p. 259). White, along with Martin (Martin & White, 2005) adopted appraisal theory to study the realisation of stance in journalistic texts through analysis of evaluative linguistic resources. Their interest lay in identifying the delicate distinctions among journalistic voices as stance revealed by 'sub-selection of evaluative options within text'...patterns of use of evaluative options within a given "key" associated with particular rhetorical objectives and the construction of authorial personae' (Martin & White, 2005, pp. 163 – 164). In this way they used appraisal theory as a method toward the analysis of stance in newspaper discourse.

Following Martin and White, Bednarek (2008) adopted the theory to analyze 'emotion talk' across corpora and suggested that appraisal not only works in SFL but also can be modified (p. 18) to develop itself with the help of other disciplinary insights. Other scholars highlighted some of the appraisal choices from appraisal theory to form new methodological frameworks for the analysis of stance or the evaluation of language in context (Macken-Horarik & Isaac, 2014; White, 2006). In addition, several researchers have found appraisal theory to be a workable analytic tool and have applied it for investigating stance operations in face-to-face conversations (Eggins & Slade, 1997; Page, 2003) and in mediated discourses (Bednarek, 2006a, 2008; Caffarel & Rechniewski, 2008; Gales, 2011; Jullian, 2011; Macken-Horarik, 2003; Martin & White, 2005; Pounds, 2010, 2012; Thomson, White & Kitley, 2008; Tran & Thomson, 2008; White, 2000, 2003, 2004, 2006, 2009; White

& Thomson, 2008).

Indeed, one of Martin and White's (2005) contributions was the application of appraisal theory to analyse the attitudinal mechanisms in putatively objective news reports, concentrating on print or online news discourse. Thus, Martin and White (2005) demonstrated appraisal theory can serve to provide an analytic perspective for revealing the ways in which stance is realised in journalistic texts, thereby showing them to be far from objective. Indeed, White (1998) used appraisal theory to identify three reporting voices in news reports and to explicate the rhetorical properties of the voice of hard news, the so-called reporter's voice. Furthermore, White (2006, 2012) provided a new framework for exploring the linguistic mechanism in hard news reporting that maintains its claim to impartiality and objectivity while nonetheless expressing attitudinal stance. Recently, Pounds (2012) expanded the application of appraisal theory from analysis of print news reporting to the multimodal analysis of television news reports. Employing the appraisal framework to the BBC news in the present research revealed the ways in which expressive choices naturalise ideologies in television news reporting through the verbal and nonverbal expression of affect.

However, little research has shown the relevance of appraisal theory for the analysis of stance provided by the discourse of broadcast news, which could thereby structure the audience's views and attitudes of the events. Appraisal theory was initially developed for analyzing the evaluative language. Some linguists have used Appraisal Theory to study print journalism because it is formally written and typically delivered via words. However, television news is delivered through different modes and modalities, conveying its meaning through verbal and visual tracks. Thus, exploring the stance of the discourse of broadcast news will necessarily involve collaborative work from linguistics, semiotics and discourse studies. Using one analytical framework would be complicated and challenging to explore comprehensively the stance of discourse in broadcast news. Therefore, this challenge and the gap in literature motivate this present study, which not only serves as an initial use of Appraisal Theory as a method to analyse the stance of the discourse of in broadcast news presentation but also complements the previous literature on television news presentation.

2.3 Review of Television News Presentation

2.3.1 Television News Presentation Defined

In basic terms, all broadcast news is dependent at some

point on a newscaster or newsreader to present or read summaries of the main news items and to link between them. As part of this role, news presentation, especially in bulletin news programs, has an important part to play as the main vehicle structuring and carrying news items within the news program. In terms of the discourse of broadcast news, though there are signs of increasingly diverse form, news presentation (Montgomery, 2007), has traditionally provided the studio-based elements of the news. At the core of these are headlines and kernels of news items. However, news presentation also includes the opening and closing of the program, shifts in the plane of discourse from kernel to subsidiary elements and back again, and of interviews with correspondents and other figures whose discourse contributes to the overall news broadcast (Montgomery, 2007, p. 68). Figure 1 shows Montgomery's (2007) proposed structure of a news item.

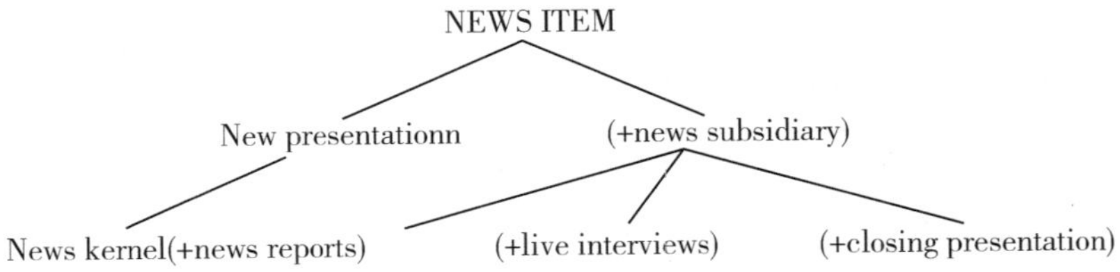

Figure 1 The full structure of a news item. In Montgomery, 2007: 52.24.

In his account, therefore, news presentation is an essential and compulsory element in structuring the overall news program as a succession of news items in the discourse of broadcast news. The presenter introduces and connects the kernel and perhaps other elements, such as (pre-recorded) news reports and interviews with correspondents and reporters in the field, to each other. Thus, as a crucial element in the discourse of broadcast news, one could regard news presentation as the most basic discourse in the unfolding of the overall news item.

2.3.2 Stance and Evaluation in News Presenter's Discourse

Television news presenters have undoubtedly been considered the central persona of television news because they not only play a salient and important part in structuring the whole news but also represent an institutional voice. Although television news presentations are the key site for expression of opinions and attitudes, only a few linguists have explored the discursive formation of this important site, in particular, the discourses produced by news presenters.

Luginbühl (2009) carried out a diachronic comparative study of news presentations in American and European TV news shows. Drawing upon a linguistic framework of text types, the researcher examined the verbal and semiotic resources of multimodal TV texts. The findings revealed that the way of presenting news was moving towards homogenization due to the technological, political and social development and the trend of 'Americanization' for European news. However, the form of news had not done so because the journalistic culture underpinning the forms of news played a key role in influencing the practices of the journalists, even though this journalistic culture was again influenced by other complex factors such as commercialization. Luginbühl's study is based on the investigation of the semiotic practices of television news presentation but failed to closely survey linguistic variation in television news presentation.

In recent years, researchers have turned to discourse analysis or linguistic analysis more generally to investigate the discourse on presenting news in television. Locating news presentation in the discursive formation of broadcast news, Montgomery (2007) illustrated the essential nature of news presentation as delivering news kernels within the overall structural of news. Although he focused much more on the formal and functional features of the discourse of news reporters or correspondents in live two-way discourse in the genre of bulletin news, he also noted that news presenters manage to structure the bulletin news items and to transition the news reporters or correspondents. He suggested that news presenters are essential to this kind of task, either explicitly by relying on lexical marking or implicitly through prosodic and paralinguistic means. This could account for news epistemology formed by broadcast news in terms of its temporal and structural framing of news programs. However, based on Goffman's (1981) participation framework, Montgomery (2007) explored the role of news presenters and their performance in detail, as well as the features of news headlines and news kernels; nonetheless, a systematic analysis of stance expressed in news reading remained somewhat underexplored in his study. After all, the news reading provides the departure of the point of views delivered by a news institution and a linguistic study of realisation of this baseline helps to better understand how institutional stance departs and varies from one context to another.

The linguistic analysis of stance in the discourse of news presenters was well exemplified in Lombardo (2009) and Ferrarotti (2009), collected in *Evaluation and Stance in War News* (Haarman & Lombardo, 2009), and their works overlap with the interests of my present study to some extent, opening the possibility of studying stance as realised across CCTV and BBC.

Lombardo (2009) and Ferrarotti (2009) evaluated

presenters' discourse in the collection of *Evaluation and Stance in War News*. Lombardo (2009) carried out a quantitative and qualitative analysis to compare data across two languages and three cultures derived from the following providers: CBS, BBC, TG5, and RAI Uno (both TG5 and RAI Uno are news providers in Italy). In the linguistic analysis, the researcher employed lexical uses and negation patterns triggered in the keyword analysis as the parameters of evaluation. The findings showed the news institutions presented Iraq war news reporting differently. For example, at times, the anchor at CBS personalised events and expressed an explicitly evaluative patriotic stance. The official source was also heavily quoted in the CBS presentation as compared with that of the BBC. The presenter at the BBC seemed to 'adopt a style of reporting typical of investigative journalism which tends to challenge official sources and which construes events as problematic' (Lombardo, 2009, pp. 69-70). Deviating from the other institutions, TG5 tended to establish a 'more explicit and closer personal relationship with viewers' (Lombardo, 2009, p. 71) and to hold a critical and negative attitude to the war. However, the other Italian news provider, RAI Uno, adopted a more traditional and balanced way of dealing with the conflicting positions and controversy. The analysis also showed that news presenters play an important role in establishing relationships with their intended audiences, which are varied given the different social-cultural contexts represented.

Ferrarotti (2009) investigated the use of terms of address (i. e., *we* and *you*) in news presenters' discourse across four sub corpora (CBS, BBC, TG5, and RAI Uno). His aim was to identify the different ways in which news presenters engage with their television viewers. A comparative analysis of the data showed that use of *we* and *you* was not necessarily identical in the communicative activities of the news presenters. The anchor at CBS played the role of reliable and detached news expert; the news presenter at the BBC was part of the news team, acting on behalf of the television audience; the news presenter at RAI Uno seemed to be a diligent teacher; and the anchor at TG5 acted as the greater interpreter.

However, the studies conducted by Ferrarotti (2009) and Lombardo (2009) provide comparisons between countries in the western context, and their examinations of stance are focused on stance realization via some particular linguistic features (e. g., the analysis of negation based on keyword analysis and the use of terms of address) in the news coverage of wars. Their studies fail to provide a more comprehensive picture of stance variation between the western and eastern context (e. g. ,CCTV vs. BBC).

In summary, this section consisted of an introduction to the relevant studies on television news presenters' discourse from a semiotic or linguistic perspective that is basically dependent on prepared text or loose scripting. In particular, some previous linguistic examinations of television news presenters' discourse (Ferrarotti, 2009; Lombardo, 2009; Montgomery, 2007) were exemplary instances for the present study that is motivated to conduct the comparison of the linguistic realisation of stance in Chinese and British television news presentations.

2.3.3 Television News Presentation as 'Reporter Voice' News

In this dissertation, I use appraisal theory as the analytic tool to explore the linguistic realization of stance in television news presentations. White's framework (2006), as is developed from appraisal theory, is adopted as the methodology for analyzing *reporter voice* news. In doing so, I treat the discourse of television news presentation as the *reporter voice* news type, following the terminology of Martin & White (Martin & White, 2005).

Initially, Martin and White (2005) identified two evaluative keys (see Figure 2) operating in print news and current affairs journalism in the English language (p. 164), identifying these keys as *reporter voice* and *writer voice* (subdivided into 'correspondent voice' and 'commentator voice') to explore the patterns of use of appraisal resources in the distinct journalistic categories of 'news', 'analysis' and 'comment/opinion'.

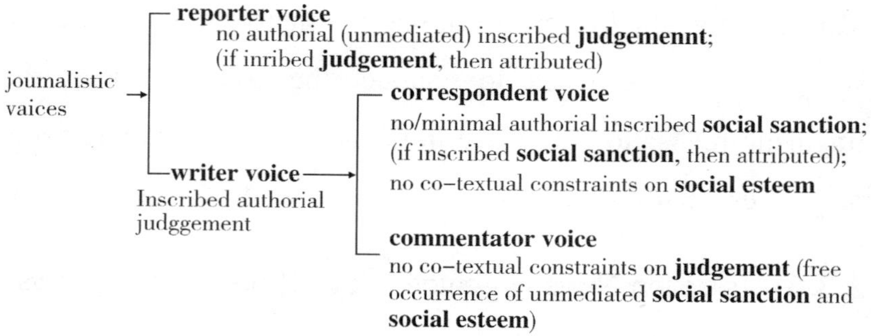

Figure 2 Journalistic keys. In J. R. Martin and P. R. R. White, 2005:173. 28

Martin and White (2005) suggested that *reporter voice* news has little or no probability of unmediated judgment; no authorial affect; and low probability of unmediated inscribed appreciation plus observed affect. Inscribed authorial **judgement** is typically identified in writer voice types of news (consisting of correspondent voice and commentator voice). Their analysis showed that the journalistic text termed *reporter* voice is most typically associated with 'hard news' coverage and the *writer voice* text is found between 'hard news' coverage and the 'somewhat less formulaic, more individualized "writing" associated with media "analysis", "commentary" and "human interest"' (p. 169). Therefore, in comparison with writer voice types of news, the *reporter voice* type appears more objective, more like 'hard news', than do *writer voice* types, such as 'commentary' or 'soft-news' reporting. *Reporter voice* news is the typical authorial stance, possibly working in a more implicit rather than explicit way.

Accordingly, not being news analysis, commentary, background information nor being 'human interest' news stories, the discourse of television news presentations is more typical of 'hard-news' (Bell, 1991; Busà, 2013) coverage because of its emphasis on timely delivery of news updates and its topicality, concerning military affairs, crimes, disasters, government statements or political issues and international concerns. Drawing upon the insights of Martin and White (2005), concerning the evaluative key, I attempted to pinpoint the key of *reporter voice* news being in conformity with the linguistic features manifest in the television news presentation.

My analysis of television news presentation was focused on highly scripted news, which has less explicit evaluation.

Although Martin and White's (2005) taxonomy of journalistic voices is based on the samples of print news discourse, which differs from the discourse of broadcast news in the modes of news delivery, the discourse of television news presentation in this study was more orally delivered and text-based; its style corresponded to Martin and White's (2005) term *reporter voice* news (p. 173) as shown in Figure 2. According to Martin and White, the *reporter voice* type of news is less explicitly evaluative, having an implicit authorial stance (see Table 2).

Table 2 Sample of Television News (News Presentation and News Report)

Boston remembered at London marathon①(sourced from CCTV news update)		
	Verbal track	Visual track
Television news presentation	Tens of thousands of runners have taken part in the London Marathon, many with **black ribbons on their vests** in honour of the victims of the Boston bombings. Hundreds of extra police officers were drafted in as part of an effort to step up security. CCTV Richard Bestic reports from London.	

① http://english.cntv.cn/program/newsupdate/20130422/100821.shtml

(续上表)

Boston remembered at London marathon[①](sourced from CCTV news update)

	Verbal track	Visual track
Television news report	*Seconds of silence* ***in tribute to the victims*** of the Boston bombing… (whistling; shouting and clapping) Most runners were wearing black armbands. So, *inevitably*, as they teemed over the marathon start line in *bright* spring sunshine, there remained *clouds of doubt* hanging in the air.	
	(VOX POP 1): "I was always going to run today but *obviously*, after what happened, it was ***so shocking*** and sort of terrible to see, so it does run through your mind -Is the same thing going to happen here today?"	
	(VOX POP 2): "***Quite worrying obviously*** and *a bit nervous about it.*"	
	London's Metropolitan Police had almost doubled the number of officers and sniffer dogs sent out to secure the event, saying this was to reassure the public and not in response to a specific threat.	

① http://english. cntv. cn/program/newsupdate/20130422/100821. shtml

（续上表）

Boston remembered at London marathon[1] (sourced from CCTV news update)		
	Verbal track	Visual track
Television news report	**In the Skies above the British capital**, a police presence also looked on. Along the entire 26 mile route from leafy Greenwich to the Tower of London, Big Ben and Buckingham Palace, litter bins had been removed as part of the enhanced security.	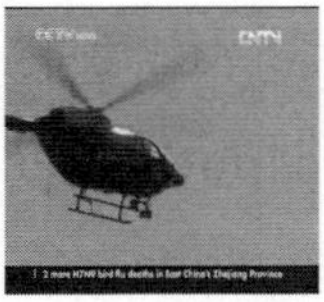
	For every one of the 36,000 runners who ***successfully*** crossed the finish line, the marathon organisers promised a MYM3 dollar donation to One Fund Boston-a total of more than MYM100,000 dollars.	
	But the *best* news was that as runners passed the finish line in London, the ***glorious day's sunshine*** was matched by the success and safety of the event.	
	They'd paid tribute to their fellow runners in Boston, raised hundreds of thousands of dollars for charity and taken part in ***a vast, colorful spectacle***. Richard Bestic, CCTV in London	

Note: The words or phrases in bold indicate the verbal information corresponding with the screen grab (in the right-handed column) in the broadcast news delivery; the italics are explicitly evaluative linguistic items.

① http://english.cntv.cn/program/newsupdate/20130422/100821.shtml

Table 2 shows the differences between television news presentation and television news report in terms of linguistic expression. First, television news presentations serve as synoptic accounts of news. In this case, the news presentation summarizes two main themes: one about the runners in the London Marathon honouring the victims of Boston Bombing and the other about the police stepping up security in London. Both news themes were discussed in detail by the follow-up news report. For example, in lines 9 – 16, the follow-up news report indicates that the runners in London Marathon were in an atmosphere of silent tribute to the victims with a sense of doubt concerning their own safety. The doubt was conveyed through the runners' attributed thoughts (see VOX POP 1 and 2). Lines 25 – 40 include the information about the police trying to ensure London's safety. Thus, compared with the follow-up news report, the news presentation provides condensed information with two sentences (Lines 1 – 7).

Second, compared to the television news report, the television news presentation is less explicitly evaluative. In the news report, authorial subjective expressions (italicized) such as *silence in tribute to the victims*, *inevitably*, *clouds of doubt*, *bright*, *so shocking*, *quite worrying obviously*, *successfully*, *a vast and colorful spectacle* and so on are explicitly evaluative. More often, these evaluative items are identified as evaluating things or expressing attitudes in various ways, such as, insertion of authorial voices (e. g., 'so, inevitably'), visual co-reference (e. g., 'seconds of silence in tribute to the victims'), and attribution to the participants in vox pop (e. g., 'shocking', 'Quite worrying obviously and a bit nervous about it.'). However, the television news presentation is more fact based than the follow-up news report, and such elements of explicit evaluation are normally restrained in the television news presentation. In short, the television news presentation summarizes news and is less subjective than the television news report.

Indeed, the linguistic features of television news presentation have also been summed up by Montgomery (2007). Compared to the other subsidiary elements of a news item in the broadcast context, such as television news reports with pre-recorded footage or live two-way interviews, the news kernel is 'a condensed summary of the key facts of a news item' (Montgomery, 2007, p. 84). Unlike a television news report from 'a reporter or correspondent featuring footage from the site of event to add information verbally and visually to that already provided by the news presenter' (Montgomery, 2007, p. 119) and the live two-way interviews described as 'the intrusion of "authorial stance" as well as features of ... "evaluation"' (Montgomery, 2007, p. 122) such as markers of propositional attitude, marked modality choices, and a greater degree of colloquial and idiomatic speeches, the news kernel carries no explicit personal point of view. Thus, as a departure of an institutional voice, the news summaries are usually authored in advance by editorial teams, and this discourse practice contrasts with the unscripted discourse in two way news interviews and the television news reports that depend on visual-verbal collaborative references (Montgomery 2007).

Projected in an institutional voice-impersonal and authoritative, television news presentations are 'synoptic account[s] of reality in which it is hard to discern a consistently identifiable evaluative position' (Montgomery, 2007, p. 87). News presenters set the discursive baseline of news, and the voices of news reporters or correspondents supplement and elaborate the discourse of news presentation. Thus, Montgomery (2007) suggested that the facticity of television news presentations is related to their 'use of unmarked modality and the absence of the speaker's point of view in the utterance: averrals that take the form of categorical assertion without obvious modal features or sharply evaluative lexis accrue to themselves the value of objectivity' (p. 87). In other words, the institutional voice of news presenters is the key tone without obvious authorial stance. Therefore, with less explicit personal attitude expressed than the discourse of correspondents and reporters in the context of broadcast news, the scripted discourse of television news presentation is more appropriately placed in Martin and White's (2005) category of *reporter voice* news in terms of the evaluative key.

Thus, television news presentations are not purely non-evaluative. Therefore, in this dissertation, I used appraisal theory, with reference to White's extended framework (2006), as the analytical tool to discover the linguistic realisation of stance provided by television news presentations. As suggested earlier, White's framework (2006), extended from appraisal theory, is methodologically appropriate for analyzing *reporter voice* news. In doing so, I treated the discourse of television news presentation as the *reporter voice* news type (Martin & White, 2005) instead of either of the other two journalistic voices.

2.4 Conclusions

This chapter contextualized the study through a review of stance studies and studies on television news presentation. First, the review addressed the notion of stance through a comparative lens to examine the existing approaches to stance studies, such as stance, evaluation, meta-discourse and appraisal. Appraisal Theory seemed to be a more appropriate approach to the present study because it offers a more comprehensive framework than the others to analyze stance in television news presentations. Second, this chapter included review of the studies on television news presentation to determine the lack of sufficient research to explore stance in the discourse of television news presentation. In addition, the chapter included discussion of the taxonomy of journalistic voices proposed by Martin and White (2005) to argue that the discourse of television news presentation resembles *reporter voice* news. Thus, appraisal theory was adopted as an appropriate analytic framework for the present study. A detailed account of appraisal theory is provided in the next chapter.

Chapter 3 Methodology and Data

3.1 Introduction

This chapter consists of two main sections. The first section concerns appraisal theory and White's (2006) extended framework, which was adopted as one of the methodological tools for data analysis. The second concerns data collection and analysis.

3.2 Brief Account of Appraisal Theory

Appraisal theory (Martin & White, 2005) is rooted in Hallidayan SFG and involves interpersonal meaning at the level of discourse semantics. With appraisal theory, one may classify discourse semantic resources construing interpersonal meanings into three systems: **attitude**, **engagement**, and **graduation**. Figure 3 is a portrayal of appraisal resources.

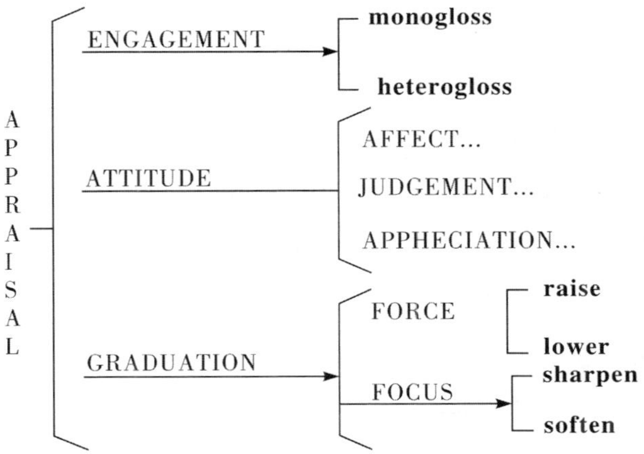

Figure 3 An overview of appraisal resources. From Martin and White, 2005: 38

Martin and White (2005) framed these three systems as separate but interacting domains. **Attitude** is concerned with feelings, including emotional reactions, judgements of behaviour, and evaluation of things. **Engagement** deals with sourcing attitude and the play of voices around opinions in discourse. **Graduation** attends to grading phenomena whereby feelings are amplified and categories blurred. Each system is further divided into different regions and dimensions.

3.2.1 Attitude

In general, **attitude** is divided into three regions of feeling (**affect**, **judgement**, and **appreciation**) in terms of three dimensions of meaning (emotive, ethic, and aesthetic).

According to Martin and White (2005),

> Affect deals with resources for construing emotional reactions...Judgment is concerned with resources for assessing behavior according to various normative principles ... Appreciation looks at resources for construing the value of things, including natural phenomena and semiosis (as either product or process). (pp. 35 – 36)

Appreciation also 'involves evaluations of semiotic and natural phenomena, according to the ways in which they are valued or not in a given field' (Martin & White, 2005, p. 43). Appraisal theory suggests that each emotion is construed by culture as binary; namely, each resource of **attitude** can be distinguished as either good or bad and as either positive or negative.

Each region in the **attitude** system may be subcategorized according to different dimensions. **Affect** can be decomposed into 'dis/inclination', 'un/happiness', 'in/security', and 'dis/satisfaction', as shown in Figure 4 below. According to Martin and White (2005), 'dis/inclination' deals with emotions of intention or volition. 'Un/happiness' deals with 'the moods of feeling happy or sad, and the possibility of directing these feelings at a 'Trigger' by liking or disliking it'

(Martin & White, 2005, p. 49). 'In/security' 'covers our feelings of peace and anxiety in relation to our environs, including of course the people sharing them with us' (Martin & White, 2005, p. 49). 'Dis/satisfaction' 'deals with our feelings of achievement and frustration in relation to the activities in which we are engaged, including our roles as both participants and spectators' (Martin & White, 2005, p. 50).

Judgement can also be encoded as either positive or negative and divided into two domains: (a) judgements dealing with **social esteem** and (b) judgements oriented to **social sanction**. **Social esteem** involves admiration and criticism without legal implications. **Social sanction** involves praise and condemnation, usually with legal implications. Judgements of **social esteem** have to do with **normality** (how special someone is), **capacity** (how capable the person is), and **tenacity** (how reliable the person is). Judgements of **social sanction** have to do with two subcategories: **veracity** (how truthful someone is) and **propriety** (how ethical someone is) (Martin, 2000, p. 156). Figures 5 and 6 show the **social esteem** and **social sanction** classifications of **judgement**, respectively.

- Affect
  - Dis/inclination
    - Fear
      (e.g. tremble,shudder,cower,wary, feaful, terrorised,...)
    - Desire
      (e.g. suggest, request, demand,miss, long for, yearn for, ...)
  - Un/happiness
    - Misery
      (e.g. whimper, cry, wail, down, sad, miserable,...)
    - Antipathy
      (e.g. rubbish, abuse, revile,dislike, hate,abhou,...)
    - cheer
      (e.g. chuckle, laugh, rejoice,cheerful, buoyant, jubilant, ...)
    - Affection
      (e.g. shake hands, hug, embrace, be fond of, love,adore, ...)
  - In/security
    - Disquiet
      (e.g. restless, twitching, shaking, uneasy, anxious, freaked out, ...)
    - Surprise
      (e.g. start, cry out, faint, startled, jolted,staggered,...)
    - Contidence
      (e.g. declare, assert, proclaim,together,confident, assured,...)
    - Trust
      (e.g. delegate, commit, entrust,comfortable with, confident in/about, trusting,...)
  - Dis/satisfaction
    - Ennui
      (e.g. fidget, yawn, tune out, flat, stale, jaded,...)
    - Displeasure
      (e.g. caution, scold,castigate,cross, bored with,angry, sick of,furious,fed up with,...)
    - Interst
      (e.g. attentive, busy, industroys,involved, absorbed,eng,engrossed,...)
    - Pleasure
      (e.g. pat on the nack, compliment,reward, satisfied,impressed,pleased, charmed,...)

Figure 4 System network for affect. Synthesized from Tables 2. 1 –5 in Martin and White,2005:48 –51.37

SOCIAL ESTEEM	Positive[admire]	Negative[criticise]
Normality 'how special?'	lucky, fortunate, charmed...; normal, natural, familiar...; cool, stable, predictable...; in, fashionable, avant garde...; celebrated, unsung...;	unlucky, hapless, star - crossed...; odd, peculiar, eccentric...; erratic, unpredictable...; dated, daggy, retrograde...; obscure, also - ran...
capacity 'how capable?'	powerful, vigorous, robust...; sound, healthy, fit...; adult, mature, experienced...; witty, humorous, droll...; insightful, clever, gifted...; balanced, together, sane...; sensible, expert, shrewd...; literate, educated, learned...; competent, accomplished...; successful, productive...	mild, weak, whimpy...; unsound, sick, crippled...; immature, childish, helpless...; dull, dreary, grave...; slow, stupid, thick...; flaky, neurotic, insane...; naive, inexpert, foolish, illiterate, unaccomplished...; unsuccessful, unproductive...
tenacity 'how dependable?'	plucky. brave, heroic...; cautious, wary, patient...; careful, thorough, meticulous, tireless, persevering, resolute...; reliable, dependable...; faithful, loyal, constant...; flexible, adaptable, accommodating...	timid, cowardly, gutless...; rash, impatient, impetuous...; hasty, capricious, reckless. l. l. l; weak, distracted, despondent...; unreliable, undependable...; unfaithful, disloyal, inconstant...; stubborn, obstinate, wilful...

Figure 5 Classifications of judgements of social esteem. From Table 2.7 in Martin and White, 2005: 53.

SOCIAL ESTEEM 'mortal'	Positive[admire]	Negative[criticise]
veracity[truth] 'how honest?'	truthful, honest, credible...; frank, candid, direct...; discrete, tactful...	dishonest, deceitful, lying...; deceptive, manipulative, devious...; blunt, blabbermouth...
propriety[ethics] 'how far beyond reproach?'	good, moral, ethical...; law, abiding, fair, just...; sensitive, kind, caring...; unassuming, modest, humble...; polite, respectful, reverent...; altruistic, generous, charitable...	bad, immoral, evil...; corrupt, unfair, unjust...; insensitive, mean, cruel...; vain, snobby, arrogant...; rude, discourteous, irreverent...; selfish, greedy, avaricious...

Figure 6 Classifications of judgements of social sanction. From Table 2. 7 in Martin and White, 2005: 53. 39

Like **affect** and **judgement**, **appreciation** can also be either positive or negative. **Appreciation** is divided into three areas of meaning: **reaction**, **composition**, and **valuation**. According to Martin (2000),

> Reaction has to do with the degree to which the text/process in question captures our attention and the emotional impact it has on us. Composition has to do with our perceptions of proportionality (composition: balance) and detail (composition: complexity) in a text/process. Valuation has to do with our assessment of the social significance of the text/process. (p. 160)

Figure 7 shows the classifications of appreciation.

SOCIAL ESTEEM 'mortal'	Positive[admire]	Negative[criticise]
Reaction: impact' did it grab me?'	arresting, captivating, engaging...; fascinating, exciting, moving...; lively, dramatic, intense...; remarkable, notable, sensational...	dull, boring, tedious...; dry, ascetic, uninviting...; flat, predictable, monotonous...; unremarkable, pedestrian...
Reaction: quality' did I like it?'	Okay, fine, good... lovely, beautiful, splendid...; appealing, enchanting, welcome	bad, yuk, nasty...; plain, ugly, grotesque...; repulsive, revolting, off - putting...
Composition: balance' did it hang together?'	balanced, harmonious, unified, symmetrical. proportioned...; consistent, considered, logical...; shapely, curvaceous, Willowly...	Unbalanced, discordant, irregular, uneven, flawed...; contradictory, disorganised...; shapeless, amorphous, distorted ...
Composition: Complexity 'was it hard to follow?'	simple, pure, elegant...; lucid, clear, precise...; intricate, rich, detailed, precise...	ornate. extravagant, byzantine...; arcane, unclear, woolly...; plain, monolithic, simplistic...
Valuation 'was it worthwhile?'	penetrating, profound, deep...; innovative, original, creative...; timely, long awaited, landmark...; inimitable, exceptional, unique...' authentic, real, genuine...; valuable, priceless, worthwhile...; appropriate, helpful, effective...	shallow, reductive, insignificant...; derivative, conventional, prosaic...; dated, overdue, untimely...; dime-a-dozen, everyday, common; fake, bogus, glitzy...; worthless, shoddy, pricey...; ineffective, useless, wrote - off...

Figure 7　Classifications of appreciation. From Table 2. 8 in Martin and White, 2005: 56.

Overall, **attitude** is to do with subjective meanings in relation to emotions and feelings and the system of **attitude** will be adopted in this present study.

3.2.2　Engagement

Engagement and **graduation**, the other two systems in appraisal, are oriented to intersubjective meanings in contexts and towards rhetorical effects from the perspective of dialogistic functionality rather than towards grammatical forms. Against the backdrop of dialogistic functionality of any utterance, the subsystem of engagement is to do with 'sourcing attitudes and play of voices' (Martin & White 2005: 35), which is concerned with the resources of intersubjective positioning. In particular, its focus is the relationships of alignment and disalignment about the value positions referenced by the text between the writer/speaker and the addressee.

Departing from the monoglossic status of an utterance, engagement involves two kinds of resources regarding heteroglossic utterances: dialogic contraction and dialogic expansion. Resources that are dialogically expansive are those that refer to any locution or utterance actively and that make allowances for dialogically alternative positions and voices, incorporating two subcategories: entertain and attribute. Resources dialogically contractive are those that refer to any locution or utterance that 'acts to challenge, fend off or restrict the scope of such' dialogically alternative positions and voices (Martin & White, 2005, p. 102). These include the subcategories of disclaim and proclaim.

Dimensions within the subcategories can also be divided into various engagement meanings (see Figure 8 below). **Disclaim** takes two forms: 'deny' and 'counter'. **Proclaim** has three: 'concur', 'pronounce', and 'endorse'. **Attribute** has two: 'acknowledge' and 'distance'. One deploys the resources of **engagement** to evaluate the interpersonal positioning indexed in the text between the writer/speaker and the addressee and to identify the interaction of the authorial voice with the readership as to whether they dis/agree, stand with, or stay away from propositions in the locutions or utterances.

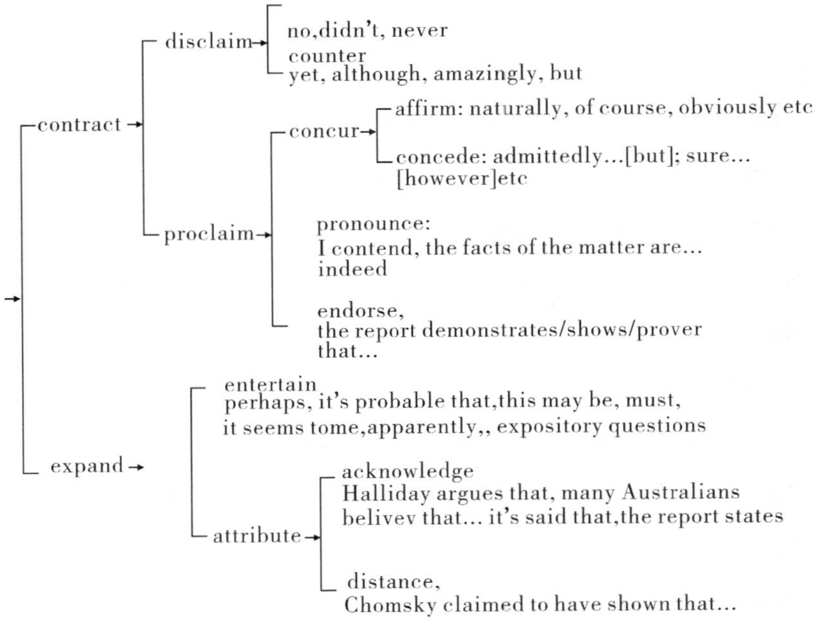

Figure 8 The taxonomy of the engagement system. In Martin and White, 2005: 134. 41

Among the sub-categories within the system of Engagement, **attribute** will be considered as one of variables for analyzing stance realized in the present study. **Attribute** roughly 'deals with the formulations, which disassociate the proposition from the text's internal authorial voice by attributing it to some external source' (Martin and White 2005:111). In appraisal theory, **attribute** is divided into two types: **acknowledge** and **distance** in terms of the use of reporting words/verbs. For example, the use of 'believe/assert' is quite different from the use of 'claim/doubt' in positioning the addressees to take up an attitude to the attributed propositions. **Acknowledge** is dialogic 'in that they associate the proposition being advanced with voices and/or positions which are external to that of the text itself and present the authorial voice as engaging interactively with those voices' (Martin & White 2005: 112). Whereas, **distance** 'involves formulations in which, via the semantics of the framer employed, there is an explicit distancing of the authorial voice from the attributed material' (Martin & White, 2005: 113). Second, 'attribute' can be distinguished from 'aver' (Sinclair, 1986) in news discourse. News utterances averred make the text monologic; news utterances attributed to other sources make the text more dialogic in terms of positioning the audiences. Therefore, **attribute** will be adopted as the appraisal resource to explore how news discourse positions audiences to take up an inter-subjective stance.

3.2.3 Graduation

Graduation is concerned with the gradability of attitudinal meanings or the upscaling and downscaling of appraisal resources. For example, the values in the three regions of **attitude** (i. e., **affect**, **judgement**, and **appreciation**) can be conveyed as greater or lesser degrees of positivity or negativity. Likewise, **graduation** is involved with the evaluation of degrees (i. e., higher or lower) of **engagement** meanings via semantics of lexis. **Graduation** deals with 'two axes of scalability—that of grading according to intensity or amount, and that of grading according to prototypicality and preciseness by which category boundaries are drawn' (Martin & White, 2005, p. 137). In terms of the former aspect, the term for graduation is 'force'; in terms of the latter, the term is 'focus'. Figure 9 shows the operation of the semantics of graduation in discourse.

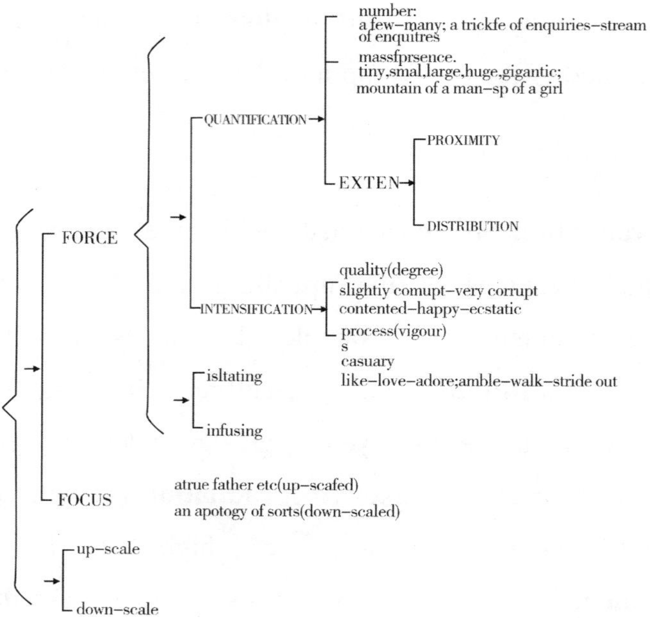

Figure 9　The taxonomy of the graduation system. In Martin and White, 2005: 154. 43

Graduation interacts with attitude and engagement in the linguistic realisation of values, positions, and stance. This is because graduation, especially force, is helpful in construing attitude and intersubjective stance through the addition of an associative effect with respect to alignment and solidarity. According to Martin and White (2005), 'Force plays another important attitudinal role in frequently acting to flag that meanings which are not explicitly attitudinal are, nevertheless, evalua-tively charged. Thus force is one of the mechanisms by which attitudinal tokens (as opposed to inscriptions) are construed' (p. 153).

To summarize, the semantic resources and subjectivity in **Appraisal** Theory are classified into three systems: **attitude**, **engagement** and **graduation**. The system of attitude and the resource of **attribute** from **engagement** will be considered as the main analytic parameters for this present study.

3.2.4 Realisations of Attitude: Inscribed and Invoked

According to Martin and White (2005), one can realise **attitude** through explicit and implicit means. Thus, appraisal resources can be divided into **inscribed** and **invoked** evaluations. **Inscribed attitudes** refer to 'evaluation that has been directly inscribed in discourse through the use of attitudinal lexis' (Martin & White, 2005, p. 61). **Invoked attitudes** occur when 'the selection of ideational meanings is enough to invoke evaluation, even in the absence of attitudinal lexis that tells us directly how to feel' (Martin & White, 2005, p. 62). Invoked attitudes express 'how appraisers want readers to feel about the appraised in a more indirect manner than "*inscribed attitudes*"' (Sano, 2008, p. 102, emphasis added). The following extract from a television news presentation is an example:

Extract 3. 2. 1 inscribed vs. invoked

> 15 people [graduation, -force, quantification] have been *killed* [judgement, -propriety] when a booby-trapped car [appreciation, -composition] *exploded* [judgement, -propriety] in a restive suburb [appreciation, -reaction] of the Syrian capital Damascus. (*CCTV News Update*, 02 – 09 – 2012)

In this example, the meanings inscribed by *booby-trapped* and *restive* are explicitly evaluative. *Booby-trap* suggests a device intended to harm or kill some people. *Restive* literally means ' unable to remain still, silent, or submissive, especially because of boredom or dissatisfaction, fidgety, restless; uneasy (OED online)' and signals the region is not in a state of easy peace. Thus, the appraised targets (i. e. , car; region) are directly inscribed and appreciated through these attitudinal lexes. The meanings encoded by the italicized elements (i. e. , kill; exploded) are neutral out of this context. However, the attitudinal positioning of these elements can be activated through factual information (i. e. , ' 15 people have been killed' by an explosion of a ' booby-trapped' car). The actions of *kill* and *explode* may trigger negative attitudinal associations. Therefore, such attitudes are invoked.

In discourse, **invoked attitude** is realised implicitly through the semantic interplay of lexis in a text. Invoked and **inscribed attitude** work together to activate readers to take up attitudinal positions. The **invoked attitude** draws readers towards the writer's position, which is explicitly expressed by the **inscribed attitude** (Chiluwa & Ifukor, 2015). As Sano (2008) noted,

> Both invoked and inscribed attitude are employed to express the writers' or a third party's evaluation of the action or phenomenon being evaluated. This evaluation can increase the chance of sharing the main arguments that are being advocated. (p. 108)

He also suggested that the inscribed attitude interplays with the invoked attitude in the texts and put this point in this way: 'on the one hand, the inscribed attitude explicitly states the ideological position of the writer with which he wants the reader to share'. (p. 108) He further commented: 'On the other hand, the invoked attitude prepares the reader to synchronize with the position expressed by the inscribed attitude'. (p. 108 – 109)

The following extract is an example:

Extract 3. 2. 2

The bill, passed by 320 to 129, follows Syria's <u>deadly *shelling*</u> [judgement, -propriety] of a Turkish town on

Wednesday. Syria has **admitted** [attribute, acknowledge] it was *responsible* [judgement,-propriety] for the *shelling* [judgement,-propriety] and has apologised [judgement, + propriety] for the *deaths* [appreciation,-valuation].—. (*CCTV News Update*,05 –10 –2012)

Here, *deadly* inscribes a negative assessment to the first reference of *shelling*; the second use of *shelling* is thus invoked accordingly in this context. *Apologise* tends to enhance the negative reading of *shelling*. Simultaneously, *death* is invoked as a negative appreciation to the bad result of the 'deadly shelling'.

Martin and White (2005) also suggested two strategies for invoking attitude, **provoke** and **invite**, as shown in Figure 10.

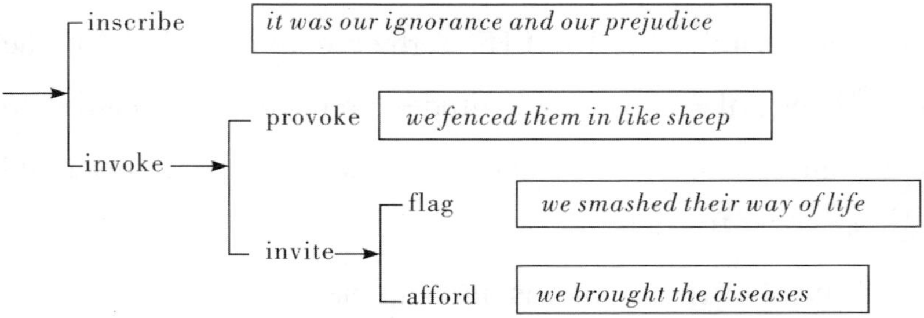

Figure 10 Strategies for inscribing and invoking attitude. Adapted from Figure 2. 3 in Martin and White, 2005:67. 46

Provoke is a strategy of indirect realisation of evaluation via lexical metaphor. The following extract is an example of this:

Extract 3. 2. 3

> UN envoy to Syria, Lakhdar Brahimi said he was scared [affect, -security] by *the weight of responsibility* [appreciation, -composition] on his shoulders. (*CCTV News Update*, 04 – 09 – 2012)

In this example, the negative evaluation of the appraised 'responsi-bility' of this mediation is provoked through the lexical item *weight* that encodes a metaphorical comparison of the responsibility Lakhdar Brahimi carries with the heaviness of things.

Invite is a strategy of indirect realisation with no lexical metaphor. It signals evaluation via other means, including counter expectation, intensification, and selection of experiential information. Invite has two sub strategies: 'flag' and 'afford'. Sano (2008) noted that the resources for counter expectation and intensification may flag the appraiser's evaluation; the resources for experiential information afford the appraiser's evaluation. Extract 3. 2. 4 is an example of this:

Extract 3. 2. 4

> While cross-border violence [judgement, -propriety] continues between Turkey and Syria, calm [appreciation, + reaction] appears to have returned to the Turkish town where five people were *killed* [judgement, -propriety]. **But** *people living* [affect, + happiness] there are still *coming to terms with* [judgement, + capacity] what's happened. (*CCTV News Update*, 07 – 09 – 2012)

Here, *coming to terms with* invokes a positive assessment of the people living in the cross-border area who are appraised as 'having kinds of capacities' via the word *but*, an expression of counter expectation, which enhances the **capacity** of the living people to go through their hard times.

White (2006) re-divided the strategies (i. e., provoking and inviting) within Martin and White's (2005) **invoked attitude** into 'provoking' and 'evoking'. 'Provoking' is an indirect realisation of the appraiser's evaluation of the appraised via rhetorical devices such as lexical metaphor, comparison, intensification, and counter expectation. 'Evoking' invokes attitude via 'experiential (factual) information' (White, 2006, p. 40). Invoked attitudes suggest non-attitudinal linguistic choices taken out of context can draw attitudinal readings as the text unfolds within a prosody established by the inscribed attitude.

3.3 White's Extended Framework

Developed from appraisal theory, White (2006, 2009, 2012) proposed a new framework or methodology aimed at evaluating the hard-news report:

> While these 'hard news' reports do typically employ a style which backgrounds or obscures the subjective, mediating role of the journalist author, thus coming across as 'objective', they nevertheless often favour particular value-laden perspectives on the events being described. Accordingly they have a clear potential to influence readers' views of these events and the attitudes they adopt towards those involved. (White, 2009, p. 30)

Hard news is the typical kind of reporter's voice text that suggests the subjective role of the author is backgrounded. The author's role is also made less salient through strategic impersonalisation, which is conditioned to be less subjective and supposedly more objective than other texts. White (2006) attempted to develop a methodology to explore the 'potential of this type of news report to function rhetorically, and ultimately ideologically' (p. 32).

Overall, the new framework as a methodology attended to two-fold meanings: (a) 'meanings where the author, by implication or association, indirectly positions the reader to adopt a particular attitudinal orientation' and (b) 'meanings by which the observations and viewpoints attributed to particular quoted sources are favoured over, or presented as more credible than, the observations and/or viewpoints of other sources' (White, 2009 p. 32).

Initially, White (2006) based the new framework on variables (such as types of attitude, agency and affectedness, and attribution) and included linguistic mechanisms 'by which attitudinal positions can be conveyed and by which the reader can be positioned to favour or disfavour a particular viewpoint' (p. 39). The new framework consists of five dimensions to observe the possibilities for variations in the mechanisms:

- types of attitude: affect, judgement, and appreciation;
- attitudinal inscription versus attitudinal tokens;
- attitudinal tokens: evoking versus provoking;
- agency and affectedness; and
- attribution.

Evaluation, which involves the three types of **attitude** (i.e., **affect**, **judgement**, and **appreciation**) is binary, either positive or negative. **Attitude** can be inscribed or invoked. Inscribed **attitude** is explicit and direct evaluation in discourse; invoked **attitude** is indirect realisation of evaluation in discourse. Inscribed attitudes not only act as sign posts to direct readers to read the attitude in their ideational selections but also interact with invoked attitudes through the prosodic realisation in discourse. In other words, **inscribed attitude** 'launches and subsequently reinforces a prosody which directs readers in their evaluation of non-attitudinal ideational material under its scope' (Martin & White, 2005, p. 64). Accordingly, White (2006) also made such a distinction between attitudinal inscription and attitudinal tokens:

> This distinction attends to the possibility that attitudinal evaluations may be more or less explicitly articulated. Attitudinal inscription applies to the use of locutions which carry an attitudinal value (positive or negative assessment) which is largely fixed and stable across a wide range of contexts .... The contrastive term 'attitudinal token' is applied to formulations where there is no single item which, of itself and independently of its current co-text, carries a specific positive or negative value. Rather, the positive/

> negative viewpoint is activated via various mechanisms of association and implication. (p. 39)

In other words, attitudinal tokens are used for formulations that are less explicitly attitudinally positioned.

Two types of attitudinal tokens exist: evoked and provoked attitudinal assessments. Evocation refers to 'those [formulations] which contain no evaluative lexis of any type ...triggering positive/negative responses by means of a focus on purely informational content...triggering positive/negative responses by means of formulations which are in other ways evaluative' (White, 2006, p. 40). Provocation means 'those [formulations] which contain evaluative material but not of an explicitly positive/negative type' (White, 2006, p. 40). White (2006) formulated the distinction between evoking and provoking tokens in this way:

> [In the case of evocation,] the positive or negative assessment is 'evoked' via purely experiential (factual) material which, as a result of being selected and brought into focus within the text, has the potential to trigger a positive or negative reaction in the reader via process of attitudinal inference. [In the case of provocation,] the positive or negative assessment is 'provoked' via material which, while

> evaluative, is not of itself positive or negative—for example, via intensification, comparison, metaphor or counter-expectation. (p. 40)

One must also consider the variables of agency and affectedness in analysing news reports. White (2006) suggested that ‘grammatical choices with respect to which participants are represented as agentive and which as affected/acted-upon often have a potential to influence who is to be seen as more to blame and who as less to blame’ (p. 40).

Attribution is an obvious feature in news reports. Through attribution, journalistic authors typically disassociate themselves from evaluative meanings, especially the more explicit ones, by attributing them to external sources. Nevertheless, a range of mechanisms exists by which journalistic authors can indirectly indicate alignment or disalignment with the externalized value position and by which the reader may be positioned to regard that position as more or less warrantable (White, 2006).

Inherited from functional linguistics, the aim of the extended framework was to apply appraisal theory to fill the gap of interpersonal function in SFL. However, White (2006) went beyond the mere annotation of **attitude** and engagement in text to call attention to the other linguistic devices of agency and affectedness, possibly manifested in the hard-news reporting style.

In sum, White's (2006) framework is essentially parameter-based and provides a means for analysing hard-news reporting style in which the overt use of evaluative meanings are relatively constrained to achieve a strategy of neutrality and impersonalisation.

However, White (2006, 2009, and 2012) employed samples from newspapers in his work, not television news data. The focus of this dissertation was the operation of stance in news reading, the news kernel of broadcast news discourse. As institutional voice, news presenters read tightly scripted news copy prepared in advance, with the news content usually being compressed and synoptic. This copy is also less explicitly evaluative and closer to hard-news reporting. Thus, the framework summarized in White (2006) seemed to offer an appropriate, practical toolkit to employ in analysing the operation of stance in television news presentations.

3.4 Data and Coding

3.4.1 Introduction to the Data

The two news programs that form the focus of this comparative study were chosen for the following reasons. First, *CCTV News Update* is broadcast in English on the CCTV international news channel several times daily. By delivering news updates in English, the program was oriented to global audiences. *BBC World News*, also directed at international audiences, launched from different areas of the world, including America and Asia. Thus, both programs were comparable in terms of their audience orientation because they were supposed to undertake the mission of profiling their institutional voices to audiences with more international cultural backgrounds.

Second, although CCTV broadcast two English news programs, *News Hour* and *CCTV News Update*, *CCTV News Update* was determined to be the more ideal counterpart of *BBC World News*, inasmuch as the program covered both international and domestic affairs. *News Hour*, the alternative English news program, aired only once daily (BJT 12:00 at noon/GMT 4:00) and mainly contained news coverage of

Chinese domestic affairs. Thus, *News Hour* was eliminated because of the difficulty in collecting news data that the BBC would also cover, making comparison of the two programs nearly impossible.

The data that comprised the two corpora consisted of the news coverage of four events that attracted wide attention between September 2012 and November 2013. The following steps were employed in the selection of data:

1. Events covered extensively by both news programs, *CCTV News Update*① and *BBC World News*, were identified to build a relatively sizeable, balanced corpus of news across the two broadcasters. Limitations in deciding what events to select included the fact that each news program was produced and broadcast in a different sociocultural context from the other to reach the intended audience of each program. While one news broadcaster actively covered some events, the other broadcaster scarcely reported those events or totally ignored them. Thus, only events covered widely on which both broadcasters focused were considered as potential data.

2. The themes of the news reports were an important factor in deciding what data were included. The themes involved various sociocultural dimensions, ranging from

① CCTV News Update was transformed into *CCTV News Desk*, a revised version of the program, as of 1 January 2015. (cf. http://cctv.cntv.cn/lm/newsdesk/index.shtml).

warfare, the political domain, the socioeconomic crisis, and terrorist attacks to catastrophic natural disasters. The multigenres of news in the data collected were expected to yield a global and comprehensive overview of the operation of stance and variations in its operation across the two culturally distinct broadcasters.

3. The news presentation corresponding to each selected news topic was extracted from the respective programs and transcribed into written text. On average, each news presentation segment was less than one minute in length. The total number of segments varied across CCTV and BBC due to different modes of programming and broadcasting. For example, the aim of *CCTV News Update* was to update the news in a timely manner and so broadcast the latest progress more than five times a day. And in the case of CCTV the wordings of the given topical event were different each time; accordingly, news segments with different wordings were selected. The *BBC World News* in Asia was usually broadcast three times a day, but the wordings of the given events were almost the same each time. Therefore, the different modes of broadcasting resulted in different quantities of news segments used as data, and for this reason, the amount of data selected from each broadcaster could vary.

Thus, the corpora for this present study were based on

television news presentation collected from the two news programs, the *CCTV News Update* and the *BBC World News*, from 2012 to 2013 where cultural and institutional contexts were quite different. The overall discourse was classified into five subsets based on the central themes of the news coverage: (a) the Syria Crisis, (b) the Eurozone Crisis, (c) the Boston Bombing, and (d) Typhoon Haiyan.

3.4.2 Description of the Data

Established for the purpose of comparison, the two corpora were collected from recordings of the TV programs broadcast from September 2012 to November 2013. Table 3 contains a summary of the data used in this dissertation.

Table 3 Data Collected by Corpora Subset

Subset	Time span (weeks)	Dates	Corpus word count	
			CCTV News Update	*BBC World News*
Syria crisis	12	01 Sept. 2012 – 31 Nov. 2012	3,834	3,714
Eurozone crisis	4	01 Oct. – 31 Oct. 2012	1,886	1,156
Boston bombing	2	16 April – 30 April, 2013	1,316	1,576
Typhoon Haiyan	3	08 Nov. – 28 Nov. 2013	1,981	1,286
Totals			9,871	8,845

The overall size of the two corpora was 18,716 words; of those, 9,871 words were from the CCTV news texts, and 8,845 words were from the BBC. The period for data collection could differ from one case to the next due to the character of the events. For example, the Syria Crisis has been an ongoing conflict since 2011 when it broke out. Other events, such as Boston bombing, were constrained in time and thus in the corresponding attention and focus on them by the media. Despite some variation in word count within each subset, the present comparative study was based on events with the intent of investigating the different attitudes held by the CCTV and the BBC for each event and their differences in reporting or representing each event.

As mentioned earlier, *CCTV News Update* is broadcast several times daily[①], while the *BBC World News* is broadcast three times daily; therefore, the frequency of broadcasting could have been a factor in the collection of the data. Because the wording of each *CCTV News Update* often varied, all the versions were included in the database. For example, in the news coverage of Typhoon Haiyan, the following two news items were aired on 10 November 2013 at different times,

① The *CCTV News Update* program is usually broadcast with updates of news for about 6 times on each workday (Monday to Friday) and more than 10 times on each day of weekends (Saturday and Sunday). (cf. http://cctv. cntv. cn/lm/newsdesk /index. shtml).

Version A from 00:00 –00:30 and Version B from 05:00 –05:30. Table 4 shows the variation in wording between the two broadcasts. In contrast, the *BBC World News* had few wording variations as the presenters for each of the daily broadcasts repeated the same news items. Therefore, only one version of each news report was included in the study data.

Table 4 Variations in Wording in Sample CCTV News Segments on Typhoon Haiyan

Version	Wording of news segment
A	The Philippine Red Cross estimates that over 1,200 people have been killed in Tacloban and Samar, the two worst-hit areas in the Philippines after super typhoon Haiyan slammed into the country on Friday. Secretary General {of the Philippine Red Cross Gwendolyn Pang, said the numbers came from preliminary reports by their teams at the two separate locations}. ①(*CCTV News Update* 10 – 11 – 2013, aired at 00:00 – 00:30)
B	Philippine President Benigno Aquino III has warned that the death toll from the super typhoon Haiyan will rise. But he adds that the government will be able to meet people's basic needs. He {has also vowed to handle the aftermath of the typhoon, saying it would be a tragedy if that were mismanaged.} ② (*CCTV News Update* 10 – 11 – 2013, aired at 05:00 – 05:30)

① From CCTV News Update, 10 – 11 – 2013, aired at 00:00 – 00:30. http://tv.cntv.cn/video/C19133/2a9f2c31717042acb6e1c4a49a19e1ed

② From CCTV News Update, 10 – 11 – 2013, aired at 05:00 – 05:30. http://tv.cntv.cn/video/C19133/7649eb69ce25428b85f54f306e5b1061

In as much as each of the broadcasters practised in a different way, their differing journalistic practice also revealed a kind of institutional stance-taking. However, this consideration was ignored because it did not seem central to the approach chosen for the present study, a linguistic analysis of the realisation of stance. However, these differing journalistic practices might have resulted in the contrast in the number of news presentation extracts collected from all the single news programs. Table 5 shows the number of data extracts collected. A total of 204 television news presentation extracts from the *CCTV News Update* were selected across all four corpus subsets; 106 extracts were selected from *BBC World News*.

Table 5 Number of Data Extracts per Corpora Subset

Corpora subsets	Number extracts	
	CCTV News Update	*BBC World News*
Syria crisis	76	47
Eurozone crisis	41	13
Boston bombing	27	19
Typhoon Haiyan	41	13
Totals	204	106

3.4.3 Data Transcription and Coding

In general, the transcription involved the main scripted discourse of news presentations, which was usually scripted in advance for delivery by the news presenters. Subsidiary discourse within the news presentation, the spontaneous speech of the news presenters as they interacted with news correspondents and other participants (i. e., interviewees or news commentators) in the news studio, was excluded from the present study. Figure 11 below shows the format used for all transcriptions. In the transcribed form of each news presentation, utterances were transcribed into grammatical clauses; punctuation marks were indicators of pauses and senses clusters. Braces indicated that although the utterance had not been completed, footage of the news report appeared on screen (such instances are also shown in Table 3).

Extract 3.4.1 (*CCTV News Update*) It's five a. m. in Beijing and welcome to the international CCTV news, I'm Yu Ze, let's meet Syria once again. Rebels have seized an air defense facility in eastern Syria. That´s according to the British-based Syrian Observatory for Human Rights. The activists said {rebels in province of Deir el – Zour overran an air defense building on Saturday--}. (02 –09 –2012)

Figure 11 Format used for transcriptions of news presentations.

Coding data in the present study consisted of attaching tags to the plain textual elements to distinguish the attitudinal resources within appraisal theory. The linguistic units (i. e., lexes, phrases, and clauses) were underlined to indicate an attitude written in the text. To distinguish one attitudinal choice from another in the text, a tag was necessarily placed after the underlined linguistic unit, as shown in Figure 12 below. The phrase *an act of terror* was underlined to show that the phrase was inscribed as an attitude in the extract. In the tag [*judgement*, *-propriety*], the brackets indicated the attitudinal system identified was **judgement** in the dimension of propriety, a subcategory of **judgement**. Because the subcategories of each **attitude** system were usually polarized, positive or negative, plus and minus signs were used to indicate the binary distinctions. The phrases underlined and italicized indicated the invoked attitudes, which invited or provoked an attitudinal response in the readers. For instance, the verbal context of the news and the news information outside the verbal texts (e. g., the injuries and deaths in Boston Marathon bombing) enabled *hailed the police response* to position the readers to take a positive evaluation of the participant U. S. president Barack Obama as a responsible president.

Extract 3.4.2 (CCTV News Update)

In response to the Boston Marathon bombing, the U. S. President Barack Obama has hailed the police response [judgement, + tenacity] and said it was still unknown [appreciation, -reaction] who was responsible [judgement, -propriety]. Speaking on Tuesday from the White House, he described the blasts [judgement, -propriety] as an act of terror [judgement, -propriety]. (17 – 04 – 2013)

Figure 12 Sample news presentation extract coded to indicate attitudinal choices.

The coding of the data in this present study was

completed according to a scheme in which several guiding criteria were used to identify evaluative linguistic units or elements in the plain text. The coding was primarily based on the vocabulary. However, some linguistic units that were invoked attitudinal resources, such as phrases invoked as attitudinal tokens, were beyond pure lexis. The process of identifying the evaluative linguistic units involved several steps. These steps will be addressed later in this section. In principle, the linguistic units in this present study consisted of three types on two linguistic levels. One type was the lexis - phrasal level, understood as explicitly evaluative resources (i.e., inscribed attitudes). The second type, also on the lexical - phrasal level, was dependent on contextual cues to position the viewer implicitly to take an attitude (i.e., invoked attitudes). The third type consisted of invocations on the phrasal - clausal level; this type relied on contextual variables and other linguistic mechanisms (i.e., rhetorical devices, metaphors, inferential associations, etc.). In the coded transcripts, invoked attitudes were indicated as underlined italics and inscribed attitudes were underlined in the normal case.

Of the two categories of units on the lexical - phrasal level, the first was directly evaluative of the semantics in the sense of the lexis explicitly arousing viewers' attitudes toward the entities. For example, words and phrases such as *crisis*, *terrorist attack*, *in memorial of*, and *celebrate* contained relatively stable positive or negative senses across texts. Thus, this type of attitude was identified as inscribed attitude.

The second category, although sometimes neutral in its own sense, resulted in viewers associating an attitude in a certain context. In the warfare report, for instance, words and phrases such as *kill*, *injure*, *deal with*, *new* and *blast*, were invoked by the elements in the context and were specifically pointed to position viewers to hold an attitude, either positive or negative. For example, to spotlight the semantic prosody of *kill* used in a preferred attitude (e. g. , negative use) in a given context, the coding unit might have been expanded to include other linguistic elements that together comprised a complete coding unit. Thus, '*killing* three people', '*wounding* more than a hundred and seventy others', and 'the *hunt* for one of the suspects' were judgements made on people's behaviours. In addition to the contextual meaning, the attitude of 'blast [n.]' is invoked/provoked due to the rhetorical device of semantic intensification. 'Blast' is defined in *Collins Cobuild Advanced American English Dictionary* (2007) as that 'a **blast** is a big explosion, especially one caused by a bomb' (p. 129). Rather than using 'explosion' or 'bombing', the choice of this word implicitly expresses an intense attitude.

The third type of linguistic unit, the phrasal-clausal level, referred to the attitude invoked in the context through larger linguistic units. This type could be evoked by the informational contents in news reports relayed through clauses (e. g., 'three people were killed'; 'a hundred and forty spectators and competitors were injured' in the Boston bombing). This type of unit has traditionally been considered informational or factual content for compliant viewers and is thus less evaluative. Invocations in appraisal suggested that these were implicitly evaluative in hard news because the attitude of the phrasal units could be evoked through their contextual cues to position viewership to take an attitude. For example, this was the coded factual description of the bomb in one news report of the Boston bombing: 'The investigators say the devices contained nails and ball bearings [appreciation, -reaction], and may have been made out of pressure cooker [appreciation, -reaction]'. Although the phrases *nails and ball bearings* and *pressure cooker* were expository composites for the making of the bomb device, they could also result in uncomfortable associations or reactions for viewers. The expository information is targeted to evaluate the bomb device (the thing) because informational contents might evoke viewers to take a negative attitudinal positioning to the bomb devices.

Sometimes, attitude of this type was provoked implicitly through different kinds of rhetorical mechanisms (e. g., metaphor, contrast, empathy, etc.). These aspects will be discussed in the chapters on the case studies. The following two coded excerpts were examples of this type of linguistic unit. In the first, 'He told me what it was like to be knocked to the ground [appreciation,-reaction] by the force of the blast. (16 – 04 – 2013)', the clause *what it was like...ground* is a description of the effect of 'the force of the blast.' In the second, 'That's a quote from him. "My thoughts," he says, "are with all those who have been affected [affect,-happiness]"', the clausal formulation *my thoughts are with all those who have been affected* serves as a compassionate expression quoted from British prime minister Cameron to the victims and is thus affective in terms of **happiness**. Different from the lexis-based attitudinal tokens, this coding unit is dependent on a larger context, which may also position viewers to take stances to the appraiser (Cameron) and to the appraised (the victims or the affected).

In practice, coding consisted of three steps. Step 1 was the coding of explicitly evaluative linguistic units that carried value-laden meanings inscribed in lexical units, (e.g., *terror*). Non-native English speaking coders could find it problematic to tell or detect some words that were explicitly evaluative. One solution to the reliability of this step was to consult dictionaries for the literal meaning of the coding units.

For example, the sense of *aftermath* in the Boston bombing excerpt was explicitly articulated in *Collins Cobuild Advanced Dictionary of American English* (2007) as 'the aftermath of an important event, especially a harmful one, is the situation that results from it' (p. 24). In the explicit sense of 'a consequence of a harmful event', *aftermath* was tagged as a negative attitudinal choice.

Step 2 was the coding of less explicitly evaluative linguistic units that reflected the value imbued within a context and invoked by its contextual reading. The neutral uses of adjectives such as *unknown*, *responsible*, and so forth were tagged as negative attitudes because these wordings were about evaluated entities targeted to the suspects responsible for the bombing.

Step 3 was the coding of implicitly evaluative linguistic units, those evoked by the factual informational content in the texts. Although the factual information itself was usually non-evaluative, it could have been associated with an attitude to evoke a viewer's response to align or disalign with the authorial subjectivity. For instance, the number of casualties resulting from a typhoon or a terrorist attack was reported in the news to position the viewers to take an attitudinal standing. The linguistic units involved were lexical, phrasal, or clausal elements in plain text and were dependent on the evaluated entities referenced in the text. The issue of data coding has been addressed in detail in each case study to justify the realisation of attitude in that study.

3.5 Conclusions

This chapter was an overview of the methodology, informed from appraisal theory and its extended framework proposed for the hard-news reporting, and the data used in the present study. The chapter contained a description of the data collected and the way in which they were collected, including the reasons for selecting *CCTV News Update* and *BBC World News* as the two programs for this examination. The news coverage of five events reported by both programs was used as sources of data for this study of the variations in stance across the television news presentations of these two broadcasters. The data were also summarised to show the building of the corpora and the transcription and coding of the data in terms of the conceptual and analytical framework.

Chapter 4 Realizations of Stance in the Television News Coverage of the Syria Crisis: A Comparative Analysis of CCTV and BBC Television News

4.1 Introduction

The Syria Crisis, also known as the Syria Uprising or the Syria Civil War, started on 15 March 2011 with demonstrations that grew nationwide and then escalated to a civil uprising, an armed clash, and an on-going conflict between forces loyal to the Ba'ath government and those wanting to replace it. The Syria conflict involved a series of military activities resulting in tens of thousands of dead and homeless. The Free Syrian Army relocated its command headquarters from southern Turkey to rebel-controlled areas of Syria from September to November 2012. On 9 Oct-ober, rebel forces seized control of the strategic town of Maarat al-Numan, which links Damascus and Aleppo. These forces were also involved with car bombings and clashes in both Damascus and Alleppo. Lakhdar Brahimi, a new special envoy to the

Syria Crisis, arranged a ceasefire during Eid al-Adhan in late October. However, the ceasefire soon broke down as both rebels and the forces loyal to the government launched a new round military attacks.

The Syria Crisis drew worldwide attention from many news institutions, including the CCTV and the BBC. This event became headline news on the CCTV and the BBC because of the nature of the event, which coincided with such news values as 'conflict' and 'negati-vity' (Montgomery 2007:7 –8). Thus, the Syria Crisis as a continuing conflict or civil war, along with its negative effects, such as large scale of casualties and fatalities, great destruction to society, and so on, made it more newsworthy to news broadcasters.

4.2 General Description of the Data

4.2.1 Data Collection and Data Sampling

This case study is based on the data collected over a 3-month period, September to November 2012. The data drew from *CCTV News Update* and *BBC World News*. The television news presentations that focused on the Syria Crisis were extracted and then transcribed into written form. *CCTV News Update* was broadcast several times a day, and each extract was downloadable from CNTV internet. *BBC World News* was broadcast three times a day; and, along with programs such as *BBC World News America* and *BBC World News GMT*, these broadcasts were recorded for data collection. Because of these differences in programming, the data extracts for each news institution varied in quantity. Data extracts included 132 CCTV news items and 47 BBC news items. Each extract lasted less than one minute. CCTV written scripts contained a total of 6,038 words in total; and the total BBC word count was 3,714.

Initial collection of the data revealed an imbalance in size between CCTV and BBC (6,038 words vs. 3,714 words, respectively); therefore, CCTV data were further sampled to make this study relatively comparable. Two situations were represented in the initial collection of the CCTV data: First, some CCTV news items occurred more than one time within one day; others occurred only once a day. The data sampling was carried out chiefly among the items appearing several times within one day, with the items with even numbers listed before them being selected. That is to say, one of every two news items was selected if that news item occurred more than once a day. Second, news items that occurred only once a day were included in the sample in a new data set. The new data set for the CCTV news contained 3,834 words and was comparable in size to the BBC data set. Table 6 shows a summary of the data collection.

Table 6 Summary of Data Collection

Program	No. of news items	Word count
CCTV News Update	76	3,834
BBC World News	47	3,714

4.2.2 A Comparative Survey of Attitudinal Resources Between the CCTV and the BBC

Both data sets were first coded in terms of the three categories of attitudinal resource: **affect**, **judgement**, and **appreciation**. Table 7 shows that the percentage for **judgement** was 60.39% of the total attitudinal resources in CCTV, followed by **appreciation** (23.38%) and affect (16.23%). In the BBC data, **judgement** constituted 48.85% of the total score, followed by **appreciation** (31.02%) and **affect** (20.13%). Thus, both data sets appeared similar in the proportional distribution of the three categories; that is, in both data sets, ***judgement*** was identified more frequently than the other two categories, with appreciation being the second highest category and **affect** the least represented category.

Table 7 Distribution of Attitudinal Resources

Category	*CCTV News Update*		*BBC World News*	
	f ①	%	*f*	%
Affect	50	16. 23	61	20. 13
Judgment	186	60. 39	148	48. 85
Appreciation	72	23. 38	94	31. 02
Totals	308	100. 00	303	100. 00

Because appraisal theory suggests that the realisation of each resource can be perceived as binary (i. e., positive or negative), binary **attitude** distributions were compared across data sets, as shown in Table 8. This revealed that in the news reports of the Syria Crisis, negative attitude exceeded positive attitude (64. 93% vs. 35. 07%, respectively, for *CCTV News Update*; 65. 34% vs. 34. 65%, respectively, for *BBC World News*). Thus, in a global sense, this event hardly surprisingly attracted negative evaluation because news relies generally on 'bad' news, which is in line with the interests of negativity as news values. This story, in this sense, is fairly typical of such kind of news because the violence and suffering brought by the Syria Crisis was against humanity and was a breach of normal human society. Ethically, people outside the news field have little chance of taking up actions to help those affected because the suffering is distant and mediated through television: the

① For the figures shown in the tables of this dissertation, the letter *f* is used to stand for 'total number'; the sign % stands for 'percentage'.

television news of Syria Crisis evokes compassion regarding the ‘distant suffering’ (Chouliaraki, 2006) of the affected among the public as spectators whether this be west or east.

Table 8 Comparison of the Positive/Negative Use of Attitudes

Category	*BBC World News* (n = 303)				*CCTV News Update* (n = 308)			
	Positive		Negative		Positive		Negative	
	f	%	*f*	%	*f*	%	*f*	%
Affect	24	7.79	26	8.44	20	6.60	41	13.53
Judgment	59	19.16	127	41.23	56	18.48	92	30.36
Appreciation	25	8.12	47	15.26	29	9.57	65	21.45
Totals	108	35.07	200	64.93	105	34.65	198	65.34

For a further examination of the operation of each of the three categories in the evaluation of text, appraisal theory suggests subcate-gorization of each category. This was done to allow examination of the different dimensions of each category to a subtle extent. **Affect** was classified into ‘un/happiness’, ‘in/security’, ‘un/satisfaction’, and ‘dis/inclination’. **Judgement** was divided into two main types: **social esteem** and **social sanction. Social esteem** was divided into three subcategories: **normality**, **capacity**, and **tenacity. Social sanction** was divided into two: **veracity** and **propriety**. As indicated previously, **judgement** was the leading **attitude** adopted by both news organizations. Therefore, further investigation was conducted to compare the aspect of **judgement** identified across the data sets. Table 9 contains a summary of these comparisons.

The five subcategories of **judgement** were evident in both data texts, and both texts prefer to use judgements in terms of propriety, suggesting that both texts were concerned with **social sanction** rather than social esteem. As shown in Table 9, the tag of **propriety** appeared more frequently than the other four subcategories. The CCTV program had 33.11% negative items; the BBC program, 25.74%. The CCTV program had 7.21% positive items; the BBC, 6.60%. We may conclude that both texts seem broadly comparable and little difference was noted among the other subcategories.

Table 9 Comparison of the Polarities of Attitudinal Resources and Associated Subcategories

Attitudes and subcategories	*CCTV News Update* (*n* = 308)				*BBC World News* (*n* = 303)			
	Negative		Positive		Negative		Positive	
	f	%	*f*	%	*f*	%	*f*	%
Affect① (50/61)								
● Security	2	0.66	16	5.25	2	0.66	27	8.91

① First number in the parentheses is the number of items from *CCTV News Update*; second number is the number of items from *BBC World News*.

（续上表）

Attitudes and subcategories	*CCTV News Update* (n = 308)				*BBC World News* (n = 303)			
	Negative		Positive		Negative		Positive	
	f	%	*f*	%	*f*	%	*f*	%
● Satisfaction	1	0. 33	1	0. 33	1	0. 33	0	0. 00
● Inclination	17	5. 57	1	0. 33	16	5. 28	2	0. 66
● Happiness	4	1. 31	8	2. 62	1	0. 33	12	3. 96
Judgment① (186/148)								
● Normality (social esteem)	10	3. 28	11	3. 61	13	4. 29	9	2. 97
● Capacity (social esteem)	6	1. 97	8	2. 62	7	2. 31	1	0. 33
● Tenacity (social esteem)	18	5. 90	5	1. 64	9	2. 97	3	0. 99
● Veracity (social sanction)	3	0. 98	2	0. 66	7	2. 31	1	0. 33
● Propriety (social sanction)	22	7. 21	101	33. 11	20	6. 60	78	25. 74
Appreciation② (72/94)								
● Reaction	8	2. 62	34	11. 15	13	4. 29	34	11. 22
● Composition	6	1. 97	5	1. 64	10	3. 30	9	2. 97
● Valuation	11	3. 60	8	2. 62	6	1. 98	22	7. 26
Totals	108	35. 07	200	64. 93	105	34. 65	198	65. 34

① First number in the parentheses is the number of items from *CCTV News Update*; second number is the number of items from *BBC World News*.

② First number in the parentheses is the number of items from *CCTV News Update*; second number is the number of items from *BBC World News*.

Propriety is used to evaluate people and the way people behave in terms of being ethically appropriate or not. As appraisal theory suggests, some people or their behaviours are morally appraised to be right or wrong and praised or condemned; therefore, the **judgement** value can be distinguished as positive or negative. A survey of the CCTV and the BBC data sets showed that negative tagging was overwhelmingly more salient than positive tagging. For example, the words like *conflict*, *bloodshed*, and *attacked* are generally indicative of ruptures of moral order. Whereas, the words such as *ceasefire*, *truce*, and *peace* are morally constructive; thus, most people accept them favourably. However, the wide use of negative **propriety** in CCTV and the BBC news coverage reflect the widespread focus on people in suffering, which could invoke the audience's sympathy and engage them in condemnation over the conflict against humanity. This also reflected the universally accepted mentality that warfare is not socially accepted by either the CCTV or the BBC. Thus, the wide use of the **judgement** value **propriety** suggested that both the CCTV and the BBC reported the events of the Syria Crisis with strategies of 'politics of pity' (Boltanski, 1999: 7), which means 'the ways in which television uses images and language to render the spectacle of suffering not only comprehensible but also ethically acceptable for the spectator' (Chouliaraki, 2006: 3). Both institutions tended to make negative moral judgements concerning the reported entities, primarily with reference to the people or the people's behaviours, in reporting the events of the Syria crisis.

4.2.3 Inscribed Tokens versus Invoked Tokens

Inscribed and invoked **attitude** are distinguished in appraisal theory (White, 2009, 2012). **Attitude** is inscribed when explicitly attitudinal lexis exists; **attitude** is invoked when attitudinal values are activated indirectly via implication, association, or optional entailment. The value of **inscribed** attitude is usually dependent on lexis that is stable and fixed in meaning; **invoked attitude** is dependent on the given context in order to be valued positive or negative.

Iedema et. al.[①] (1994) analysed the different generic texts (i. e., hard news, human interest stories, comments, and features) in newspapers and distinguished three different authorial voices: 'reporter voice', correspon-dent voice, and commentator voice. 'Reporter voice' means 'no explicit judgement, yet tokenised **judgement** and indirect **judgement** by means of non-core items allowed'. Correspondent voice is involved with 'explicit **social esteem** judgment', and

① Cited in http://grammatics.com/appraisal/MediaLit-Appraise.pdf

commentator voice refers to both explicit **social esteem** and explicit **social sanction** judgements (Iedema et. al 1994: 308).

Based upon insights from White (2009, 2012), the distinction between **inscribed attitude** and **invoked attitude** was applied in the text coding of the Syria Crisis. The following extracts from both the BBC and CCTV news data sets have been presented to exemplify the coding of attitude.

Extract 4. 2. 1 (*BBC World News*)

> The <u>new</u>① [invoked: judgement, + normality] UN envoy to Syria, Lakhdar Brahimi, says Syrian government must respond to the **legitimate** [inscribed: judgement, + propriety] demands of its people. On Mr. Brahimi's first official day in his post, Syrian government announced that forces **loyal** [inscribed: judgement, + tenacity] to president Assad have repelled **a large scale attack** [inscribed: judgement, -propriety] by rebels on an air force college near the city of Aleppo. Meanwhile, Jordan has issued a joint call with the UN's refugee agency for seven-hundred million dollars in order to <u>help</u> [invoked: judgement, + propriety] care for the <u>growing</u> [invoked: appreciation, -reaction] number of refugees

① Note: The attitude invoked are designated by the elements underlined in order to be distinguished from the attitude inscribed highlighted in bold.

from **the fighting** [inscribed: judgement, -propriety] in Syria. More than a hundred and eighty thousand Syrians are currently **in shelter** [inscribed: judgement, -propriety] in Jordon, many of them at specially constructed [invoked: appreciation, + reaction] camps. A little earlier I asked UN Higher Commission for Refugees spokesperson in Jordon, Andrew Harper, whether the number of Syrian refugees had taken his organization by **surprise** [inscribed: affect, -security]. (02 – 09 – 2012)

Extract 4. 2. 2 (*BBC World News*)

The Jordanian government has nearly doubled [invoked: judgement, + capacity] its estimates of the amount of money it needs to **cope with** [inscribed: judgement, -capacity] the influx of refugees [invoked: appreciation, -reaction] from Syria. In an **appeal** [inscribed: affect, -satisfaction] issued jointly with the United Nations, Jordan says it **urgently needs** [inscribed: affect, + inclination] seven-hundred million dollars. More than a hundred and eighty thousand [invoked: judgement, -normality] Syrians are **currently sheltering** [inscribed: affect, + security/judgement, -propriety] in Jordan. The country is struggling [invoked: affect, -security] to meet their needs. Gale Gavlick reports from Amman. (02 – 09 – 2012)

In these two BBC extracts, inscribed tokens in bold were obviously evaluative; and the meaning of these tokens is stable independently of their contexts (e. g. , the lexis *legitimate*, *loyal*, *attack*, *appeal*, *refugees*, and [*in*] *shelter*). Those, either lexis or words, which are value-laden in their semantics, were thus treated as inscribed attitude. The underlined tokens were less explicitly evaluative and became attitudinal only within their given contexts. For example, *new*, a relatively neutral term in its semantic meaning, provoked an evaluative meaning in the first utterance describing the person Lakhdar Brahimi, who took a new position as an envoy to Syria, in comparison with the failure of the old envoy (i. e. , Kofi Annan) to mediate the crisis. Invoked **attitude** was realized by formulations such as 'to help care for', 'doubled its estimates of the amount of money', and 'influx of refugees'. Invocations or attitudinal tokens usually project evaluation via association or entailment to extend their positive or negative prosodies. For example, 'double its estimate of the amount of money' was coded as a **capacity** of **judgement** because evaluation was made concerning the decision or action of the Jordanian government and its association with a **capacity** to do so at least on the level of social esteem. 'Influx of refugees' evoked negative feeling via the aggregate meanings of *influx* and *refugee*. Thus, the negative meaning of the inscribed 'refugee' was extended. In this sense, the **invoked attitude** was realized.

Similar tokens were also found in the CCTV data sample, as shown in these examples:

Extract 4.2.3 (*CCTV News Update*)

Good morning from Beijing, you are watching CCTV news, I'm Yu Ze, let's go to the latest in Syria now, 15 people [graduation (force), quantification] have been killed [judgement, -propriety] when **a booby-trapped** [appreciation, -composition] car exploded [judgement, -propriety] in a **restive** [appreciation, -reaction] suburb of the Syrian capital Damascus. (02-09-2012)

Extract 4.2.4 (*CCTV News Update*)

He (Ban Ki-Moon) also **warns** [affect, -security] Syrian government about the uses of chemical weapons [judgement, -propriety], that's **a big concern** [affect, -security] of the western capital. —. The UN Secretary-General says the use of such weapons [judgement, -propriety], if it would happen, would be "**an outrageous crime with dire consequences** [judgement, -propriety]." (02-10-2012)

Extract 4.2.5 (*CCTV News Update*)

The city of Homs **suffered** [affect, -happiness] **fresh**

> **shelling** [appreciation,-reaction] on Saturday, according to amateur video posted online. Elsewhere, activists [judgement,-propriety] claimed that civilian homes in Daraa had been **set alight** [judgement,-propriety] by forces **loyal** [judgement, + tenacity] to Syrian President Bashar Assad. (02 – 09 – 2012)

In these extracts, the sense of words such as *kill* (Ex. 4.2.3) was supposed to be neutrally understood beyond this given context. However, when '15 people' are involved in the killing, the word *kill* as a reported factual element results in the audience associating it with the immoral consequence of the act of killing, people's death, and even to associating the dead people with innocent ordinary residents. The reporting fact of '15 people have been killed' in this sense invoked regarding the car bombing, which was negative and immoral. In Extract 4.2.4, 'the use of such weapons' was coded as a negative attitude of judgement, along with propriety, because 'the use of such weapons' referred to 'the use of chemical weapons' in the preceding sentence. This formulation invoked a feeling of condemnation of the action in using weapons to kill people. Moreover, the negative meaning inscribed in the attitudinal token *crime* (Ex. 4.2.4) was semantically intensified with modifiers such as 'outrageous' and 'with dire consequences'. Another case from Extract 4.2.5 was *shelling*, which semantically entailed ‘heavy fire’ or ‘explosive’, which could lead to destruction of the social order. This word was explicitly negative in its meaning and showed the journalist's emotional rejection; thus, it was negatively appreciated. The word *fresh* in ‘fresh shelling’ carried one of the interests of news value-RECENCY, and seemed to indicate a subtle intensification of this negative cue. The intensification of negative **appreciation** revealed sympathy toward the civilians in the city of Homs. However, the reporting verb *claim* had the effect of distancing the authorial voice from the activists. In this context, ‘activist’ was negatively coded as judgement.

4.3 Attribution as Realization of Stance

Another characteristic in the discourse of television presentation was the use of attribution (i. e., attributing the statement or the news proposition to an external source or reporting news information by quoting another source). Attribution is one of the strategies journalists adopt as part of the strategic ritual of doing objectivity. As a rhetorical device in news discourse, attribution has been discussed in previous studies (Piazza, 2009; White, 2012). Piazza (2009) used corpus linguistics to examine attribution, addressing its frequency in the use of other voices, identities attributed, various modalities of represented discourse, and the type of verbs employed, among others. Based on appraisal theory, White (2012) treated quoted source descriptors (i. e., the naming and designation of sources) as having the potential to invoke attitude. Notably, both researchers emphasised the *sayer* in the attribution. Thus, 'who *says* what' is very important in the process of attribution. The following sections concern the framing and expressing of news propositions and the *sayer* in both data sets.

4.3.1 Identification of Reporting Verbs/Words

Table 10 shows the reporting words/verbs identified from each text. A wide range of reporting words were found across both data sets. These words included verbal nouns (e. g., *statement*, *announcement*), verbal phrases (e. g., *say/saying*, *report* (*v.*)/*has the report* (*n.*)), and adjuncts (e. g., *according to*). The data indicated that the present tense of the verb *say* was widely adopted in news texts from both programs and that words and phrases such as *report* and *according to* were preferred by both programs. Reporting words such as *describe*, *acknowledge*, *tell*, and *witness* (verb) were found in the BBC texts but not in the CCTV texts. Words such as the past tense of *say* and *state/statement* occurred more frequently in the CCTV texts than that in BBC texts.

In terms of rhetorical functions, uses of words like *say*, *report*, and *according to* seemed neutral in attitude to the attributed proposition. However, uses of words such as *describe*, *witness*, *acknowledge*, *tell*, and *admit* in the BBC news program seemed to acknowledge external sources. In particular, *witness* was more supportive and assertive in the degree of evidential stance, as is shown in the following three extracts:

Extract 4. 3. 1 (*BBC World News*)

Our world affairs correspondent Ian Pannell and cameraman Darrel Conway are among the few western journalists to have *witnessed* the start of the battle in Aleppo in July. They've now returned to the city from where they sent this report. (09 – 10 – 2012)

Extract 4. 3. 2 (*BBC World News*)

The BBC's Ian Pannel along with camera man Don Conway have *witnessed* firsthand the horrors of life under fire there. (12 – 10 – 2012)

Extract 4. 3. 3 (*BBC World News*)

The extent of the suffering has been *witnessed* by a BBC team in one of the city's hospitals where doctors are struggling to treat large numbers of people including children. (12 – 10

–2012)

In these extracts, BBC correspondents were identified as the experiencing witnesses in the news report, establishing an alignment between the news presenter and the correspondent with reference to the evidentiality of the news proposition, indicating the source of the information was their direct observation.

Table 10 Occurrence of Reporting Words

Reporting words	*CCTV News Update* (n = 91)		*BBC World News* (n = 89)	
	f	%	*f*	%
Say/saying	28	30.77	33	37.08
Said/have said	27	29.67	6	6.74
Claim/claiming	3	3.30	1	1.12
Show/showing	2	2.20	2	2.25
Propose/be proposed	3	3.30	1	1.12
Announce/announcement	1	1.10	2	2.25
State/statement	6	6.59	1	1.12
Describe	0	0.00	4	4.49
Admit	0	0.00	2	2.25
Acknowledge	0	0.00	2	2.25
Report/has/sent the report	13	14.29	25	28.09

(续上表)

Reporting words	*CCTV News Update* (n = 91)		*BBC World News* (n = 89)	
	f	%	*f*	%
Tell	0	0.00	2	2.25
Witness (v.)	0	0.00	3	3.37
According to	8	8.79	5	5.62

The uses of *claim*, *state*, and *propose* seemed to be creating distance from the external source. The different use of the words reflected the journalist's attitude toward the external source, as shown in the following extracts for the word *claim*.

Extracts 4.3.4 (*CCTV News Update*)

Elsewhere, activists ***claimed*** that civilian homes in Daraa had been set alight by forces loyal to Syrian President Bashar Assad. (02 – 09 – 2012)

Extracts 4.3.5 (*CCTV News Update*)

In the meanwhile, in the same part of the world, the Syrian rebels say they have captured a helicopter base 15 kilometers east of Damascus after an overnight battle. It is the second military facility they have ***claimed*** to have captured on the outskirts of the Syrian capital this month. (26 – 11 – 2012)

In these cases, the news journalist used the word *claim* with the external sources activist and Syrian rebels. By distancing the proposition, the journalistic attitude seemed to be distancing rather than acknow-ledging (Martin & White, 2005). Thus, the activist and Syrian rebels were less aligned with the journalists.

4.3.2 A Comparison of Sayer Between the CCTV and the BBC

As indicated previously, White (2012) discussed the potential of quoted source descriptors as attitudinal invocations and suggested that several cases function to evoke attitudinal assessments. Source descriptors may include those without 'accompanying modifications but naming high status international figures and perhaps some religious leaders' (p. 60) and those which 'reference high profile organizations' (p. 60). He also pointed out that 'in cases where the named source is not widely known, then additional descriptors as to the source's profession, institutional membership, position in a hierarchy and so on may become attitudinally charged.' (p. 60) However, White did not clarify how such attitudinal invocations are defined and specified but merely suggested that 'the potential of such formulations is entirely contingent, dependent on co-textual conditioning and the beliefs and attitudes the reader brings to the text' (White, 2012, 60).

Thus, the text of the Syria Crisis was examined to identify the differences between the CCTV and BBC programs in the way source descriptors may evoke attitudinal potentials.

The use of *say* in both data sets showed that reporting verbs such as *say* or *report* usually follow a source of the propositions, the *sayer*. The *sayer* may be one of three categories of voice: voice as an individual social agent, voice as group in a plural form, and voice as an institution/organization. The proposition voiced from the *sayer* as an individual contrasts with one from the *sayer* as a group or institution because of the apparent transition of attributing the news proposition from a specific and transparent source to a general and less transparent one in terms of its evidential status.

The voices referenced by the word *sayer* in the data for this study have been displayed in Tables 11 and 12.

Table 11 Identification of the Sayer in CCTV News Update Texts (n. =55)

Accessed voice	*f*	%	Instances
Individual social agent	29	52. 73	●The new UN envoy to Syria ●He (UN Secretary-General Ban Ki-moon) ●Paulo Pinheiro, an expert leading the UN's team of human rights investigators ●The UN Secretary-General ●Turkish Prime Minister Tayyip Erdogan ●His spokesman
Plural social agent	13	23. 64	●UN investigators ●Activists ●Witnesses ●Syrian activists ●The Syrian rebels ●The activists; etc.
Official institution/ organization	13	23. 64	●The Syrian Network for Human Rights ●Syria's state TV ●The Syrian Observatory for Human Rights ●Syria's state-run news agency SAN ●The Damascus Governorate ●It (the Syrian government) ●The Syrian Observatory for Human Rights ●A Syrian opposition group ●The Syrian national Council; etc.

As shown, the *sayer* could refer to an individual social agent, some people from a group, or some institution or nation. In the CCTV texts (Table 11), 52. 73 % were voices from individual social agents who were referenced directly (e. g., Lakhdar Brahimi, Ban Ki-moon, and Turkish Prime Minister Tayyip Erdogan). With this form of reference, news presenters make the degree of certainty of the attributed proposition more transparent by reference to its source. Institutions or official organizations and plural social agents were each identified as the *sayer* in 23.64% of the instances in the data.

In the BBC data (Table 12), the voices from an individual social agent, a plural social agent, and an official institution/organization were equally distributed, respectively with the similar ratios of 30.78%, 33.33% and 30.78%. Therefore, the BBC seemed to prefer not to use an individual's voice as *sayer* in attribution. As for the voice from an individual social agent, no close co-references were found between the person and the individual's corresponding official rank or social status. This contrasted with the CCTV data in which that voice was tied strongly with wording indicating the individual's social role, thereby validating the quoted proposition in the complement clause.

In terms of communicative function, the three types of voice seemed different in the degree of transparency and evidential status in information delivery. The more general the voice is, the less transparent the source of information is to the viewer. In this sense, CCTV was inclined to attribute news statements more transparently by specifying the *sayer* as individual social agent.

Table 12 Identification of the Sayer in BBC World News Texts (n. =39)

Accessed voice	*f*	%	Instances
Individual social agent	12	30. 78	● The new UN envoy to Syria, Lakhdar Brahimi ● He (Ole Solvang is emergency research at Human Rights Watch) ● General Robert Mood ● A Syrian government official ● Turkey's Prime Minister ● Mr. Brahimi ● UN envoy Lakhdar Brahimi ● The BBC's Jim Muir ● He (French Foreign Minister Laurent Fabius) ● Rasmussen
Plural social agent	13	33. 33	● Syrian activists ● Activists ● Activist groups ● Opposition activists ● Turkish authorities ● Opposition sources ● Opposition forces ● Syrian opposition fighters ● Rebel sources

（续上表）

Accessed voice	*f*	%	Instances
Official institution / organization	12	30. 78	●United Nation's children's agency ●Jordan ●The UN refugee agency ●Aid agencies ●The UN ●the US ●The Syrian military ●Save the Children
Unspecified	2	5. 13	●Is it fair to say ●If it's actually just being realistic or saying

Notably, most of the agents categorised as voice from an individual social agent were identified with official titles or social ranks (e. g., 'the Ambassador to Tehran Leon Jagarian', 'Turkish Prime Minister Tayyip Erdogan', 'The EU's Foreign Policy Chief Catherine Ashton'). This formulation strongly suggested the social role played by the *sayer* and thus foregrounded the social status of the *sayer*; what was said by the *sayer* was backgrounded in the flow of information. The speech function of this kind of formulation is to support what is stated persuasively and to work as evidence in the presentation of the quoted information. Evidential status hidden in the institutional discourse becomes more enhanced than the practice of including the verbal quotations from the other two types of *sayer*s. This practice featured in CCTV can be contrasted with that in BBC. Table 12 showed that news statements in BBC are equally attributed to the three categories of individual social agent, plural social agent and official institutions. However, compared with CCTV text, the *sayer* as individual social agent lacks a strong correspondence between the individual person and his/her social status (e. g., Turkish Prime Minister Tayyip Erdogan vs. Turkey's Prime Minister).

The comparison also showed that CCTV preferred to attribute news propositions to specific persons in their news reports rather than to certain groups of people or institutions; whereas the BBC tended to balance the different types of verbal quotations. This difference revealed that the accessed voices (Hartley, 1982, 1992, 2002) were subject to professional mediation in the journalistic practice. CCTV was disinterested in the pursuit of information transparency in news quotations and was less balanced in its choice of quoted voices; the BBC tended to be impartial in balancing a wide range of voices.

4.3.3 Functions of Say in the Comparative Contexts

The verb *say* in both the CCTV and BBC data usually appeared early in the utterances, prior to the complement clauses (i. e., the attributed news propositions). The functions of *say* in different contexts indicated different speech acts across the data sets. In CCTV, 'X say Y' was a proclamation of something to the audience and seemed to be declarative and authoritative in its context. The *sayer* was usually identified by some lexis, which might also bear some socially marked status. However, in the BBC news, the structure of 'X say Y' seemed to state something to the audience, functioning as evidence and support for the preceding or posted propositions. The following examples were included to elaborate this point:

Extract 4.3.6 (*CCTV News Update*)

Now let's (later) on the Syrian Crisis, speaking at a news conference after meeting a number of Egyptian leaders in Cairo, Lakhdar Brahimi *-the UN and Arab League special envoy to Syria*-said that there will be "no miracle" solution to ending the crisis in **Syria**. (11 – 09 – 2012)

Extract 4.3.7 (*CCTV News Update*)

Syria's state-run news agency SAN says a car bomb has killed 27 people and wounded more than 60 in the northern city of Aleppo. Fire trucks tried to extinguish the blaze as [rescue workers dug through mounds of rubble]. (10 – 09 – 2012)

Extract 4.3.8 (*CCTV News Update*)

Turkish Prime Minister Tayyip Erdogan says parliamentary authorization of deployment of Turkish troops is intended solely as deterrent. (05-10-2012)

In these examples, the italics are the identification of the *sayer*s. The *sayer* 'Lakhdar Brahimi' (Ex. 4.3.7) was followed by an identifier, 'the UN and Arab League special envoy to Syria', before the verb *say*. The function of the phrase 'the UN and Arab League special envoy to Syria' was to identify the social role of the *sayer*, which might associate what he said with the source's social obligation; thus, his social role could bring the audience a sense of trustworthiness. In Extract 4.3.8, the phrase 'Syria's state-run news agency' was identified with 'SAN' as a quoted source. The *sayer* was introduced in a formal way, preceding what the *sayer* said; this also formalized the attributed news proposition by enhancing the formality of the speech in a communicative context. In Extract 4.3.9, the source, Tayyip Erdogan, was preceded with his official status, 'Turkish Prime Minister', thus authorising the attributed speech of his personal voice to be a national declaration.

Interestingly, as shown in the following extracts from the BBC news data, the sayer was not identified in such a way, although it might evoke an emotion.

Extract 4. 3. 9 (*BBC World News*)

A little boy, one of the thirty seven thousand people who have been killed in the course of this conflict. And as the violence continues in Syria, there has been more diplomatic fall out over a passenger plane flying from Moscow to Damascus that was intercepted by the Turkish air force yesterday. Turkey's Prime Minister says the plane was carrying Russian-made military equipment and munitions. Our Turkish correspondent James Reynolds has the details. (12 – 10 – 2012)

Extract 4. 3. 10 (*BBC World News*)

As the conflict in Syria also goes on, Europe may consider lifting an arms embargo, that's according to French Foreign Minister Laurent Fabius. He says that France will discuss the option with its European partners, now that an opposition coalition has been established. It comes as the UK's national security council meets today to consider military, humanitarian and diplomatic options for dealing with the on-going crisis. Well, in our studio in central London is Shashank Joshi who is a research fellow at the Royal United Services Institute. (15 – 11 – 2012)

In both cases, the *sayer* was not modified and the attribution of what X said was naturally extended from the preceding utterances. No particular emphasis was placed on the identification of the *sayer* in the expression, and the focus was fixed on the content of what was said. For instance, 'Turkey's Prime Minister' only referred to the sayer, with little hint to the specific person (i. e., Tayyip Erdogan) who held the official position of prime minister in Turkey. In short, the structure of 'X say Y' in BBC functions to state news information, which contrasted with CCTV news in which the function of 'X say Y' in the discourse was only to proclaim statement.

4.4 Agency and Affectedness: The Representation of Casualties in the Syria Crisis

In news practice, journalists commonly report what happens to people; thus, 'who does what to whom' is often the essential way of representing an action reported in the news. Interestingly, when reporting the activities of conflict, the usual practice is to identify who the victims may be and to address in what way and in what numbers people are dead or injured in the conflict. However, the way these are represented in the news discourse may position the audience to take an attitudinal orientation or may even reflect journalistic preferences or ideologies. For example, many critical analysts (Billig, 2008; Fairclough, 2003; Fowler, 1991; Fowler et al., 1979) have examined the linguistic features of news representation and suggested that the use of nominalisation and passive voice over the use of verbs and active voice is ideological. Nominalisation and passive voice result in transforming the process of action into an abstract entity and in deleting the agency. Doing so may result in excluding participants and thereby in the linguistic creation of a thing.

This section contains the examination of the discourse of casualties, specifically their representation in the news texts from this study. The people involved with the representation of casualties typical had the roles of agency and affected.

Based on textual observation, casualties were reported via the verb *kill*. However, the CCTV and the BBC used that verb differently in their reporting of the Syria Crisis. Both the CCTV and the BBC usually represented *kill* as a result instead of as an action, as shown in the following examples:

Extract 4.4.1 (*BBC World News*)

Activists say about a hundred people have been killed in the latest violence across the country. (09-09-2012)

Extract 4.4.2 (*BBC World News*)

At least ten people have been killed when a car bomb exploded in the northern Syrian city of Aleppo. —Many of the victims were killed in air strikes, which also destroyed a major water pipeline in Aleppo. (10 – 09 – 2012)

Extract 4.4.3 (*CCTV News Update*)

Now, 15 people have been killed when a booby-trapped car exploded in a restive suburb of the Syrian capital Damascus. (02 – 09 – 2012)

In these instances, agent in the act of killing becomes absent through the use of passive voice of *kill*. The avoidance of its agent had the effect of turning the act of killing into a factual result of the violence. In the news reports, the victims were generally depicted as innocent people and were dead because of the violence or incident. In this journalistic standing, the deaths of common people were not directly ascribed to any party in the violence; or it may also be the case that who exactly is the agent is not clear. This invoked an emotion of sympathy over the victims while also repressing a feeling of moral condemnation or criticism over the doer of killing. For example, one of the victims who was '**a little boy**' was the focus of the journalist in the news utterance, 'A little boy, one of the thirty seven thousand people who have been killed in the course of this conflict (*BBC World News*, 10 – 12 – 2012), thus invoking sympathy for victim. However, the doer in the killing and the intention of killing were overshadowed by the violent incident and thus remained understated or unsettled for the audience. This kind of factual report seemed to be objective but weakened the journalist's standing towards the fact of killing innocent people.

In addition, the verb *kill* usually co-occurred with words such as *conflict*, *violence*, and *attack* or with specific references of incidents such as *air strike* and *car bomb*. Such wording resulted in intensifying the causal relationship between the lives of people claimed and the happening of these events. However, this bonding also resulted in blocking the identification of the doer in the act of killing.

Table 13 shows some of the subtle differences between the CCTV and the BBC in the use of *kill*. The basic meaning of *kill* is 'to put to death; to deprive of life; to slay, slaughter' (*OED* online); it is a transitive verb that can be used in both active and passive forms. Although *kill* was usually agentless in both corpora, the different treatments by the CCTV and the BBC in terms of its active or passive uses resulted in different meanings. As shown in the table, both the CCTV and the BBC used the verb in both active and passive voices, with the

CCTV somewhat preferring the active voice to the passive and the BBC preferring the passive.

Table 13 Use of Active and Passive Voice for the Verb Kill

Program	Active voice	Passive voice
CCTV News Update	9	7
BBC World News	3	12

The following extracts from the BBC data show the uses of *kill* in different contexts:

Extract 4.4.4 (passive form; *BBC World News*)

> Activists say about a hundred people have been killed in the latest violence across the country. Jim Muir reports now from neighbouring Lebanon. (09-09-2012)

Extract 4.4.5 (passive form; *BBC World News*)

> On to other news now. At least ten people have been killed when a car bomb exploded in the northern Syrian city of Aleppo. State-run TV aired footage that showed destroyed buildings and rescue workers trying to pull people from the rubble. Activist groups say that more than a hundred and sixty people died in the latest fighting in the country. Many of the victims were killed in air strikes, which also destroyed a major water pipeline in Aleppo. Jim Muir reports now from

neighbouring Lebanon. (10 – 09 – 2012)

Extract 4.4.6 (passive form; *BBC World News*)

General Robert Mood says that kind of engagement risks militarizing the conflict even further. Eighteen months of violence have already seen thousands killed, and many more fleeing to the camps in neighbouring countries. Our correspondent has the story. (12 – 09 – 2012)

Extract 4.4.7 (active form; *BBC World News*)

In any case, Turkey has already retaliated to a Syrian mortar attack which killed five people at a border town. (04 – 10 – 2012)

Extract 4.4.8 (active form; *BBC World News*)

The UN Security Council has come to a rare agreement on Syria, condemning in the strongest terms the Syrian mortar attack which killed five people in the Turkish border village area. — (BBC world news, 05 – 10 – 2012)

In passive voice, the verb usually takes the form of 'X people were killed in Y', with X standing for the number of people and Y standing for the violent incident. Usually, the reporting of casualties in each item of news was a relatively complete and independent syntactic expression. These complete expressions stated the facts of deaths, de-emphasising the agents. When a cause-effect relationship was taken between the death of a mass of people and the conflict incident, the result was reported prior to the cause, and thus the result was foregrounded in the BBC news. Syntactically, the less frequent use of *kill* in the active voice was usually bound with other propositional elements in the attributive clause adjunct to the main clause. The speech served to supplement the main body of information in the utterance.

The use of *kill* in active voice in the BBC data differed from that in the CCTV news data. The following examples show the discourse function of the active form found within the CCTV data:

Extract 4. 4. 9 (*CCTV News Update*)

According to a Syrian activist group, forces loyal to Syrian President Bashar al-Assad have killed at least 25 men after shelling a village in Hama province. (03 – 09 – 2012)

Extract 4. 4. 10 (*CCTV News Update*)

A Syrian opposition group says a suicide car bomber has killed at least 50 Syrian government troops, in what would be one of the bloodiest single attacks on President Bashar al-Assad's forces. (06 – 11 – 2012)

Extract 4.4.11 (*CCTV News Update*)

> Meanwhile, Turkey's Foreign Minister Ahmet Davutoglu, says that a shell fired into Turkey on Wednesday, killing five people, could only have come from forces loyal to Syrian President Bashar al-Assad. (07-10-2012)

As shown, *kill* used in the active voice was more common than the use of its passive voice and it was usually framed with a reporting utterance, which had relatively direct references identifying the doers of killing (e. g., 'forces loyal to Syrian President Bashar al-Assad' and 'a suicide car bomber'). In addition, the use of *kill* in active included two types: as a verb in a clause (*kill*) and as a predicator in a non-finite clause (*killing*). The predicator *killing* in a non-finite clause occurred four times in the data and was used in constructing the description of violent incidents, such as the car bomb or shell. This way of representing casualties was different from that representation in the BBC news as complete factual elements.

The active use of *kill* in the CCTV foregrounded the process of the act of killing, allowing the presenter to emphasise the brutal nature of the violent action for the audience's perception. As stated earlier, the doer in this form was usually identified and associated with that person's brutality. The use of *kill* in passive voice was usually buried in the BBC's utterance, functioning to report the factual element of the violence. By doing so, the affected was foregrounded and the doer was backgrounded, inviting the spectator's compassion for the death and injuries instead of condemnation over to the doer.

4.5 Conclusions

Based on White's (2006) framework, the examination of this case study revealed the way in which stance was linguistically realized in television news coverage of the Syria Crisis by the CCTV and the BBC. First, the variation of **attitude** was not marked between the CCTV and the BBC. Both CCTV and BBC tend to take a negative stance towards the event of Syria Crisis in their textual realization; this negative attitude was associated with **social sanction**. To be specific, the **propriety** in **judgement** stood out as the most salient choice among all the attitudes, indicating that both institutions regarded the Syria Crisis as a breach of the moral order and thus attached judgement to the people or their behavioural activities in terms of normative moral values. However, this kind of attitude also suggested a sense of condemnation for those responsible for the people trapped in the suffering. In addition, insecurity as **affect** was captured in the news reports, inviting a response from the audience in terms of 'suffering in a distance' (Boltanski, 1999). Moreover, unlike other news genres, for both institutions, most of the evaluative resources were implicitly conveyed via contextual associations or entailments, invoking emotional reactions, either positive or negative.

Second, although attribution, a strategy to maintain the objectivity of the news, was adopted by both the CCTV and the BBC, subtle differences on the level of linguistic expression existed. The range of reporting words adopted by the CCTV was less than that of the BBC. Apart from the use of *say*, *report*, *according to*, both institutions tended to exploit other words differently. The CCTV news tended to exploit *claim* and *propose*, displaying a neutral stance to the external source. The BBC used reporting words such as *describe*, *witness*, *acknowledge*, *tell*, and *admit*, showing an authorial voice engaging with external sources. In addition, the *sayer* as source descriptor was identified as one of three types in terms of the degree of transparency and certainty of the attributed propositions. However, the *sayer* in the CCTV data was identified with social status or official rank, making the reporting verb *say*, with its the reported proposition, more declarative. In comparison, data showed the BBC featured *say* as supportive and evidential in its discourse function.

Finally, in the discourse of casualties, both the CCTV and the BBC used an agentless structure, thus avoiding representation of the agenct of killing. However, the uses of the active and passive voices in relation to *kill* by the CCTV and the BBC revealed their different attitudes towards the relationship between casualties and the violent incidents: although both CCTV and BBC emphasize the process of killing, CCTV is more likely to identify the agent of action than BBC who tend to leave the agent uncoded by the use of the passive voice with agent deleted.

Generally speaking, therefore, we can see that there is no strikingly divergent in the adoption of attitude resources between the CCTV and the BBC; and both of them are likely to evaluate the death and the casualties involved in the warfare by relying on the choice of **judgement**. However, the CCTV tends to take up a distancing position to interact with the external sources whereas the BBC seems to engage interactively with the external sources.

Chapter 5 Realizations of Stance in the Television News Coverage of the Eurozone Crisis: A Comparative Study of CCTV and BBC Television News Presentations

5.1 Description of the Data

The Eurozone Crisis, also known as the Euro Crisis, attracted the attention of journalists worldwide when it broke out in the Eurozone in 2009. The data for this analysis consisted of the television news coverage of this crisis. The Eurozone Crisis involved the disruption of life in the socioeconomic domain, affecting many countries and leading to various responses at the state or government level as well as to reactions among ordinary people. For this reason, comparing the different ways in which journalistic institutions mediated and represented this disrupted reality warranted investigation. The data for this case study were collected from the CCTV and the BBC over the one-month period of 1 – 31 October 2012. The data included 41 news extracts containing a total of 1,891 words from CCTV and 13 news extracts with a total of 1,156 words from the BBC.

The aspects of appraisal theory (Martin & White, 2005) as described in the preceding chapters served as the basis for comparing the ways in which **attitude** was distributed across these two news data sets. Table 14 contains an overview of the attitudinal resources drawn upon by both news organizations. In a global sense, both institutions showed a preference for **judgement**, although no big discrepancies in terms of frequency of use were found in the distribution of the three choices. The dominant category adopted for each broadcaster was different. It was '**appreciation**' for CCTV, using it in 40.51% of the instances found and it was '**affect**' for the BBC, using it in 36%.

Table 14 Comparison of Attitude Resource Distribution

Resource	*CCTV News Update*		*BBC World News*	
	f	%	*f*	%
Affect	35	22.15	36	36.00
Judgment	59	37.34	34	34.00
Appreciation	64	40.51	30	30.00
Totals	158	100.0	100	100.0

The attitudinal resources adopted were not the same for both the BBC and CCTV, and differences were noted in the frequency of using each resource. The BBC data set revealed little difference in the frequency with which **affect**, **judgement** and **appreciation** were used. CCTV, however, showed a distinct preference for using **appreciation** over **affect** (40.51% vs. 22.15%, respectively).

5.2 Distribution of Attitude Polarity

The distribution between positive and negative attitude is shown in Table 15. Overall, **attitude** in the CCTV data (53.79%) tended to be more positive than negative, for the majority of the positive attitude are adopted to the organizational aids or efforts to solve Eurozone Crisis; whereas in the BBC data (47.00%), the reverse was true. **Judgement**, 'construing attitudes to people and the way they behave' (Martin & White, 2005, p. 52), was a common concern in the evaluation mechanism for both data sets.

Table 15 Comparison of the Polarity of Attitudinal Resources

Resource	CCTV News Update				BBC World News			
	Positive		Negative		Positive		Negative	
	f	%	*f*	%	*f*	%	*f*	%
Affect	17	10.76	18	11.39	17	17.00	19	19.00
Judgement	39	24.68	20	12.66	19	19.00	15	15.00
Appreciation	29	18.35	35	22.15	11	11.00	19	19.00
Totals	85	53.79	73	46.20	47	47.00	53	53.00

Both institutions also held positive attitudes toward the people and their behaviours relating to financial support and rescue solutions for the Eurozone Crisis. These coded examples were taken from the data: (a) '[Spain will] meet its state deficit reduction goals' (CCTV, 2012 – 10 – 02); (b) '[EU member states to] support the poorer regions' (CCTV, 2012-10 – 10); and (c) '[Top of the agenda is] how to get the global economy growing more rapidly' (BBC, 2012 – 10 – 10). These extracts were identified as involving the judging of people's behaviours in struggling with this crisis, although the evaluated targets were usually represented as states, governments, or organizations rather than individual persons.

Another parallel situation was the negative appraisal of **appreciation** in both sets of data. This indicated that objects, processes, and people's performance had become the negative targets in the texts. These resources were anchored in expressions such as 'economic consequences hit by the crisis' (e. g., 'The Eurozone jobless rate hit a record high', CCTV, 2012 – 10 – 02; 'Spanish economy is going to shrink', CCTV, 2012 – 10 – 10); 'the Eurozone economy has contracted', CCTV, 2012 – 10 – 04; 'the debt crisis erupted', BBC, 2012 – 10 – 09) and 'austerity measures' (e. g., the Spanish government's program of austerity has been controversial,

BBC,2012 – 10 – 09). Indeed, these discourses underlie the issue of the metaphorical representation of the crisis. The situation of the Eurozone economy was metaphorically represented as a crisis through such terms as *hit*, *shrink*, *erupted* and *contracted*. Indeed, the words indicate physical actions with the meanings transferred from a concrete cause-effect relationship, that is, something that gave rise to the Eurozone crisis. These metaphors suggested that the Eurozone economy was a physical object, such as a patch of cloth shrinking or contracting from such external forces as washing or drying out. However, the causes that gave rise to the effect-the crisis-are implicit.

A further examination of the **attitude** operating within the data sets of the two institutions involved the subcategories of each of the **attitude** resource. Table 16 shows the data for the three categories of attitude. Affect in the CCTV data was mainly involved with the subcategories of **inclination** (10.13%) and **satisfaction** (5.70%), which indicated the consequences of the Eurozone Crisis brought about negative responses in the thread of **satisfaction** but positive responses in the mental behaviour of **inclination** related to coping with the crisis. The negative responses are relevant to 'protest', 'student's strike' and etc., which express dissatisfaction of government's announcements. For example, 'thousands of secondary and university students have protested [affect,-satisfaction] across Spain against education cuts. ' Additionally, the positive response in relation to coping with the crisis focused on 'request' for aid, for instance, 'a request for European aid' was positively coded in the sentential context of 'Spanish Prime Minister Mariano Rajoy has said a <u>*request*</u> [affect, + inclination] for European aid is not imminent'. Here the activity of 'request' was closely bound with the solutions of crisis.

Table 16 Comparison of Polarity in the Subcategories of Attitude

Resources and subcategories	*CCTV News Update*				*BBC World News*			
	Positive		Negative		Positive		Negative	
	f	%	*f*	%	*f*	%	*f*	%
Affect								
●Security	0	0.00	7	4.43	1	1.00	8	**8.00**
●Satisfaction	1	0.63	9	**5.70**	1	1.00	7	7.00
●Inclination	16	**10.13**	0	0.00	12	**12.00**	0	0.00
●Happiness	0	0.00	2	1.27	3	3.00	4	4.00
Judgement								
●Normality	1	0.63	8	5.06	1	1.00	9	**9.00**
●Capacity	8	5.06	3	1.90	3	3.00	1	1.00
●Tenacity	19	**12.03**	2	1.27	6	6.00	0	0.00
●Veracity	1	0.63	1	0.63	2	2.00	2	2.00

（续上表）

Resources and subcategories	CCTV News Update				BBC World News			
	Positive		Negative		Positive		Negative	
	f	%	*f*	%	*f*	%	*f*	%
● Propriety	10	6.33	6	3.80	7	7.00	3	3.00
Appreciation								
● Reaction	12	7.59	26	**16.46**	6	6.00	12	**12.00**
● Composition	13	8.23	8	5.06	1	1.00	4	4.00
● Valuation	4	2.53	1	0.63	4	4.00	3	3.00
Totals	85	53.79	80	46.21	47	47.00	53	53.00

Note: the figures in the table was highlighted in bold for comparison.

Affect in BBC is similar to CCTV in terms of **inclination** adopted. Here is a case extracted from the BBC data: 'European leaders will try [affect, + inclination] to bridge over differences [judgement, + tenacity] over plans for a banking union during the summit'. Here the word *try* was correlated with the act of bridging over differences and was positively coded because it showed a strong mental process for the sensor 'European leaders' as well as potentially inviting viewers to take a positive orientation toward European leaders' acts. In addition, emotions about the Eurozone crisis in the BBC data concerning the dimension of **security**were negatively represented. In this instance, 'It also says that investors are most worried about [affect,-security] the viability of the Euro zone [appreciation,-composition; balanced] and the state of the U. S. government's finances [appreciation,-composition; balanced]', the formulation of '[be] most worried about' could arouse a negative attitude for viewers that will potentially take an evaluative position in this case. In terms of **judgement** in both news corpora, people and their behaviours were frequently evaluated along with **propriety** (positive and negative) with around 10% in both CCTV and BBC data sets, which concerns the norms of ethics in a given social-cultural context, For instance, *protest* or *protester* in any stable socioeconomic context should be regarded as a breach of social norms or as people with inappropriate behaviours without reference to the rationality of their requests and appeals. Thus, *protester* is inscribed as a negative **judgement** of those people who protest. Likewise, in the coded utterance 'Spanish people to make donations to help [judgement, +propriety] their compatriots', the act of making a donation and offering help were taken as positive **judgement** of people's behaviour.

Judgement was also performed within the area of social esteem. Apart from **propriety**, in BBC data, the **judgement** was also adopted along with the dimension of normality, which coloured the 'EU winning Nobel Peace Prize' to be absurd in this context of Eurozone Crisis.

In the CCTV data, **judgement** was realised by **tenacity** to the extent of 12.03% to render ' how dependable or reliable the people or their behaviour is', which concerned the reliability of financial organizations such as ECB and IMF. For instance, in ' she says she expects **courageous** [judgement, + tenacity] and co-operative [judgement, + tenacity] action on the part of IMF members' (CCTV, 2012 - 10 - 11), both *courageous* and *co-operative* were used to describe positively how resolute the action of the IMF members would be. Moreover, positive evaluation with regard to **tenacity** was preferred to its opposite. Thus, **judgement** along this line was largely concerned with the first campaign launched by the Spanish Red Cross to raise funds to help crisis-stricken people, potentially evoking an emotion or perception of the gravity of the Eurozone Crisis and thus orienting the viewers to take a particular attitude toward the event.

In the BBC data, **normality** was the main dimensions for **judgement** in the area of **social esteem. Normality** is associated with how special the people and the behaviours are. A case from the BBC exemplifies this usage ' [A] s we've been reporting, the Nobel Committee has **awarded** [judgement, -normality] this year's Peace Prize to the European Union. The decision has started a heated debate [judgement,-normality] across social media as to whether it's the right [judgement, +propriety] call'. And another example follows, ' This is the only way to explain the **absurdity** [judgement,-normality]'. In the BBC, **normality** was adopted largely in relation to the Nobel Prize awarded to EU, explicitly evaluating the Nobel Prize awarded to EU being special as 'absurdity'.

Negative **appreciation** was cast along with **reaction**. Thus, economic problems such as ' Eurozone crisis', ' economic setbacks', and ' risks to financial stability worldwide' could result in audiences taking negative positions in regard to the Eurozone Crisis.

5.3 Attribution

Attribute is one of the resources used in dealing with intersubjective stance (Martin & White, 2005). First in this section is an examination of the different attitudes held in dealing with the rhetorical device of attribution as a resource in constructing intersubjective stance. A comparative examination of BBC and CCTV texts suggested some differences with respect to the use of this strategy. In addition, the two subcategories of **attribute**, **distance** and **acknowledge**, have been examined. These subcategories indicate whether the authorial voice stands with the proposition, with the distinction being made via the choice of framer or the reporting verbs.

5.3.1 Attribution in the BBC and CCTV Data Sets

Attribution, in comparison with the notion of averral (Sinclair, 1986), is characterised by a framer or a reporting verb placed between an internal idea or an utterance and an attributee or an external source. In investigating the BBC and CCTV data sets, differences in the adoption of attribution were found between the two organizations. Table 17 shows these findings.

Table 17 Distribution of Attribution

Organization	No. of clauses	No. of attributed propositions	%
CCTV	161	66	40.99
BBC	153	19	12.42

The communicative value of attribution is often assumed to be that of 'mak[ing] the speaker or writer remain aloof from, and unimplicated in, any of the value positions which are contained in attributed material' (Martin & White, 2005, p. 115), thus making text more objective and impersonalised. Only a few cases of attribution (19 or 12.42%) were identified in the BBC data. Of those, only seven were attributed to the external voice in the overall text. The CCTV data contained 66 (40.99%) news propositions with attributions to external sources. The lesser use of attribution by the BBC indicated that the BBC tended to instil much subjectivity, even assertive stance, in the events reported. In contrast, the wide use of attribution in CCTV news communications could potentially make the overall discourse more open and dialogically expansive. In this sense, the BBC tended to aver news information to the audience; whereas the CCTV attempted to attribute news propositions to the external resources. However, this point was beyond the stated expectations for this research.

5.3.2 Attribution or Averral-Like Statements

Another distinction in the discourse of attribution between the CCTV and the BBC involved averral-like statements. The pattern of attribution in the BBC texts contained more averral-like statements; the attribution in the CCTV texts included both attributions and averral-like statements. Hunston (2000) explained that if an utterance or thought is attributed, it is derived from some other source than the writer or speaker presenting the material; if an utterance or thought is averred, the writer or speaker is speaking for him/herself. A proposition that is identified as being given by a third party through the use of reporting words such as *say*, *report*, and so forth is called an attribution. If a proposition is stated directly by the writer or presenter him/herself, with no reporting words, then it is an averral. The following examples are illustrative of these distinctions:

Extract 5.3.1 (*CCTV News Update*)

> 'Well, the German Chancellor Angela Merkel says Europe needs clear intervention rights when member states' national budgets violate EU rules'. (18 – 10 – 2012)

Extract 5.3.2 (*hypothetical instance*)

> 'Well, Europe needs clear intervention rights when member states' national budgets violate EU rules'.

In the first extract, the proposition 'Europe needs clear intervention rights when member states' national budgets violate EU rules' was attributed to 'German Chancellor Angela Merkel'. This extract was considered an attribution. The second extract shows the transformation from attribution to averral. The writer uttered this statement and made no mention of any external source.

Despite these distinctions, attributions and averrals remain connected. In principle, a writer must assume responsibility for what is attributed while also delegating responsibility for what is attributed to the source (Sinclair, 1986, as cited in Hunston, 2000, p. 178). Hunston (2000) also suggested a more complex relationship exists between attribution and averral because attribution is usually embedded in averral and averral may be modified by modals or by vague language to become attribution. That is to say, the border between attribution and averral could be blurred if one ignores the what or the who being evaluated in the discourse. For example, in Extract 5.3.1, 'the German Chancellor Angela Merkel' was the external source of the attributed proposition as well as the appraiser of the proposition, the **judgement** maker of the actions carried out by European Union member states. As the appraiser, 'the German Chancellor Angela Merkel' also reflected the writer's stance, indicating that 'German Chancellor Angela Merkel' was believed to be a socially and consciously biased agent but a reliable source and thus shared in the responsibility for the proposition attributed. This attribution example (Extract 5.3.1) shows the writer's willingness to align with the source to present the attributed proposition.

Another possible distinction also exists between attribution and averral in the case of material attributed to a source that is inherent with epistemological truth, as shown in

Extract 5. 3. 3：

Extract 5. 3. 3（*BBC World News*）

The latest IMF figures predict the Spanish economy is going to shrink [appreciation, -composition] by 1. 3 percent next year.（10 – 10 – 2012）

In this case, 'the latest IMF figure' was the source of the proposition attributed by the use of the verb *predict*. *Figures* might arouse an association with mathematical operations, which are based on objective knowledge. In this sense, the source could be evaluated as true in knowledge (by the speaker or writer). The knowledge might even be commonly held as objective and true by both the writer and the viewer). Compared with a social agent such as 'Angela Merkel' as an externalised source, the 'IMF figures' seemed to be more internalised in the writer or speaker's truth of knowledge. If so, the overall utterance would be more like an averral even though it includes a reporting verb.

Up to now, the source descriptors have been appraised as one of two kinds in terms of degree of the source's subjectivity and the certainty of the source's knowledge: social subjects and social objects. Indeed, this phenomenal distinction has already drawn the attention of some scholars. Bednarek

(2006b) suggested that a gradience already exists between **attribution** and '**based averral**', pointing out that 'attribution is based on what Sayer or Senser said or thought (HE said that), whereas the based averrals can be premised on the writer's interpretation of data (a poll—showed that/Tests found)' (p. 647). However, the BBC data suggested the need for the concept of averral-like statements rather than Bednarek's (2006 b) '**based averral**'. As shown in the following extracts, the BBC texts were more complex than appeared in the initial observation of those data:

Extract 5. 3. 4 (BBC World News)

> **The International Monetary Fund** says there have been new setbacks in attempts to nurse the world economy back to recovery. The IMF has now lowered its forecast for global growth to just over 3% for this year and next. **It** says the main problem is that economic policy in developing economies has failed to rebuild confidence. **It** also says that investors are most worried about the viability of the Euro zone and the state of the US government's finances. James Kelly has more. (09 – 10 – 2012)

In this item, the attributed source was an organization, 'The International Monetary Fund', which is different from both the externalised source as a socially and consciously biased agent and any interpretation of the data. Rather, it is some object between the two. The truth value contained in what this object says is higher than that expressed by an individual social agent but lower than the interpretation of bare data. Epistemological positioning of this kind diverges from that contained in attribution, tending to converge with that in '**based averrals**'. An averral-like statement is a third type that includes utterances that are between attributions and '**based averrals**'. Thus, the patterns of attribution presented in the following examples (attribution in Exs. 5. 3. 5 – 9 and averral-like statements in Exs. 5. 3. 10 – 15) were identified as averall-like statements.

Extract 5. 3. 5 (attribution; *CCTV News Update*)

Europe's commissioner for monetary affairs, Olli Rehn says Spain will meet its state deficit reduction goals.

Extract 5. 3. 6 (attribution; *CCTV News Update*)

Spanish Prime Minister Mariano Rajoy has said a request for European aid is not imminent.

Extract 5. 3. 7 (attribution; *CCTV News Update*)

Spain's Economy Minister, Luis de Guindos, has said

a "bad bank", set up to allow lenders to offload bad investments, will be 55 percent privately owned.

Extract 5.3.8 (attribution; *CCTV News Update*)

European Commission President Barroso calls on the more prosperous EU member states to support the poorer regions at the Friends of Cohesion summit in Bratislava.

Extract 5.3.9 (attribution; *CCTV News Update*)

But **Greek Finance Minister Yannis Stournaras** said the talks were going well after the troika meeting.

Extract 5.3.10 (averral-like statement; *CCTV News Update*)

The Governing Council of the ECB also decided that the interest rates on the marginal lending facility and the deposit facility will remain unchanged at one point five percent and zero percent respectively.

Extract 5.3.11 (averral-like statement; *CCTV News Update*)

The ECB (European Central Bank) has announced it will keep its main interest rate unchanged at a record low of zero point seven five per cent.

Extract 5.3.12 (averral-like statement; *CCTV News Update*)

Figures released earlier in the day show the Eurozone

economy has contracted further at the end of the third quarter this year.

Extract 5. 3. 13 (averral-like statement; *CCTV News Update*)

The IMF's Global Financial Stability Report has indicated that a combination of lower risk appetite, a weaker global economy and of course continuing risks in the Euro area have led to increased macroeconomic risks [judgement, -propriety] for the entire global economy.

Extract 5. 3. 14 (averral-like statement; *CCTV News Update*)

The IMF has forecast that the Spanish economy will contract by 1. 3 percent next year -more than double its previous predictions.

Extract 5. 3. 15 (averral-like statement; *CCTV News Update*)

The Financial Times reports that a legal opinion prepared for finance ministers says the plan to create a single Eurozone banking supervisor is illegal. It says EU law does not permit such changes in how the ECB works.

Identification of the social actors in the source descriptors as variables to invoke **attitude** was attempted in the previous case analysis of Syria Crisis. In the present case analysis, the focus was on the communicative function of attribution and averral-like statements. As suggested in appraisal theory, attribution can be read as distancing or acknowledging stance via the choice of the framers or reporting verbs. Hunston (2000) also accepted this: 'One of the functions of the choice of report verb is either to leave open the option of disagreement with attributed statement (e. g. , *argue*) or to preclude such disagreement (e. g. *point out*)' (pp. 185 – 186).

In the CCTV examples, the reporting verbs were more diverse, including not only verbs such as *say* and *call on* in the attributions but also verbs such as *decide*, *announce*, *show*, *indicate*, and f*orecast* in the averral-like statements. All these reporting verbs could be grouped into the **acknowledge** subcategory of attribution, indicating agreement with the attributed statement. However, the more diverse use of reporting verbs in averral-like statements showed more authorial solidarity to the source descriptors than the use of *say*, a more neutralised stance marker. This naturally corresponded with the use of source descriptors. In the averral-like statements, these descriptors were *organization* and *figures*, which were more or less inherent with higher epistemological positioning than the social agents with biased mentalities. Hence, the authorial alignment with the external source was likely established; and the voices (authorial voice and source's voice) tended to be converging and homogeneous in the sense of communicative functions.

On the other hand, compared with attribution, averral-like statements were not as preferred in the CCTV data, which contained only 6 instances out of the total of 27 with a ratio of 22.22%. Thus, although CCTV used both types of strategic devices in dealing with attributed materials, CCTV news remained a dialogically expansive voice. CCTV's preference for attribution to the averral-like statements suggests that CCTV news are open to possibilities of engaging external voices rather than to close down such possibilities with an authorial voice.

The BBC examples have also been grouped according to the distinction between attribution (Exs. 5.3.16 – 17) and averral-like statements (Exs. 5.3.18 – 22):

Extract 5.3.16 (attribution; *BBC World News*)

Stephen Evans is **our man** in Berlin and **he** says that the **German press** thinks that Greece should remember where this bailout money has come from.

Extract 5.3.17 (attribution; *BBC World News*)

The director of the IMF's monetary capital markets Jose Vinals has been speaking in the past few hours. **He**

outlined what the IMF believes must be done in the Eurozone.

Extract 5. 3. 18 (averral-like statement; *BBC World News*)

The International Monetary Fund says there have been new setbacks in attempts to nurse the world economy back to recovery. (BBC, 2012 – 10 – 09)

Extract 5. 3. 19 (averral-like statement; *BBC World News*)

It (The International Monetary Fund) says the main problem is that economic policy in developing economies has failed to rebuild confidence. (BBC, 2012 – 10 – 09)

Extract 5. 3. 20 (averral-like statement; *BBC World News*)

It (The International Monetary Fund) also says that investors are most worried about the viability of the Euro zone and the state of the U. S. government's finances. (BBC, 2012 – 10 – 09)

Extract 5. 3. 21 (averral-like statement; *BBC World News*)

It's (**IMF's**) warned that the risks to financial stability worldwide have risen in the past six months, and despite efforts to resolve the Eurozone debt crisis the region is still seen as the main risk to global financial stability. (BBC,2012 -10 -10)

Extract 5. 3. 22 (averral-like statement; *BBC World News*)

The latest IMF figures predict the Spanish economy is going to shrink by 1. 3 per cent next year. (BBC, 2012 -10 -10)

Of these extracts, five were averral-like statements; only two were attributions. Thus, the BBC seemed to favour averral-like statements more than the CCTV. All of the source descriptors were either ' Internal Monetary Fund (IMF)' or the ' IMF figure (s)'. IMF is an international organization with a long history, since 1945, and is described as ' an organization of 188 countries, working to foster global monetary cooperation, secure financial stability, facilitate international trade, promote high employment and sustainable economic growth, and reduce poverty around the world' (IMF). Referencing the IMF confirmed and enhanced the attributed propositions because the IMF is an organization associated with positively reliable and true values. As suggested previously, the higher epistemological stance indicated in the source descriptors possibly converged with the authorial voices and thus made the averral-like statement more declarative and even more authorial.

The BBC also projected an authorial intervention to the attributions. The first example contained an embedded pattern of attribution. The proposition 'Greece should remember where this bailout money has come from' was originally attributed to the 'German press'. Then the attribution of 'German press thinks' was again reported by another source, 'he', referenced as 'our man'. The alignment with the source 'he' reflected an authorial acquiescence to the attribution 'German press thinks'. In the second example, 'he', the source of the proposition 'what the IMF believes must be done in the Eurozone', was identified as 'the director of the IMF's monetary capital markets Jose Vi? als'. What Jose Vi? als did was averred, totally in authorial voice, with the following attribution working only as complementary information. Thus, the attribution as a device of dialogic functions was discursively subject to an authorial intervention.

Overall, the BBC data indicated less preference for the use of attribution. Although limited uses of attribution were employed, these attributions were patterned more as authorial interventions. Thus, the textual features characterising the discourse of the Eurozone crisis were more proclaiming, dialogically contractive (Martin & White, 2005), and even assertive. In contrast, CCTV rested on attribution, which was split into two types, attribution and averral-like statements, in terms of the epistemological positioning of the source descriptors. Attribution was still the type favoured by CCTV, although averral-like statements were also found. This comparison indicated that CCTV tended to take more intersubjective stance to the Eurozone Crisis in terms of a dialogic dimension and the BBC was more inclined to directly engage with the Eurozone Crisis through averring the news.

5.4 Agency and Affectedness: The Discourse of Austerity in the Presentation of the Eurozone Crisis

The Eurozone Crisis remained not only a socioeconomic issue but also a rather complicated one that evoked a series of social reactions, and austerity measures on a range of levels, from governments to average citizens. Thus, an examination of the reporting and representation of austerity in the news discourse of the BBC and the CCTV was warranted. In a general sense, if taking austerity measures to rescue Euro Crisis is an activity of tension in a series of news reports, the agency of this action will naturally fall on the part of governments as governments play a role in pushing austerity measures. The affected are supposed to be ordinary people who tighten their belts in their daily lives.

To make the analysis comparative, this exploration was undertaken through investigating the semantic prosody through which austerity was communicated across the CCTV and BBC news programs. The notion of semantic prosody (Sinclair 2003) was suggested as essential in better understanding the meaning of a word used in 'a particular cotext, which carries extra meaning of an emotive or attitudinal nature' (p. 117).

Austerity, one of the prominent themes in overall news discourse, may also result in connotative meanings across collocational formulations. The following extracts show how meanings of austerity with different collocations may vary:

Extract 5.4.1 (*BBC World News*)

> This visit is intended [affect, + inclination] to **show support** [judgement, + tenacity] for the Greek government as it attempts to push [affect, + inclination] through **the tough austerity measures** [appreciation, -composition] to cut its deficit [judgement, + propriety]. On the eve of this, though, thousands of demonstrators [judgement, -normality] have been on the streets. They've been **chanting anti-austerity slogans** [affect, -happiness] and warning [affect, -security] Angela Merkel that she's **not welcome** [affect, -happiness] in their country. From Athens, Mark Lowen has more. (BBC, 09 – 10 – 2012)

Extract 5. 4. 2 (*BBC World News*)

The Spanish government's programme of austerity [judgement, -tenacity, neutral] has been **controversial** [appreciation, -reaction] and it has led to hundreds or maybe even thousands of demonstrations [judgement, -normality]. (09 - 10 - 2012)

Extract 5. 4. 3 (*BBC World News*)

The Greece, she'll see this time around is mired in recession [appreciation, -composition] and its people **angry about** [affect, -happiness] the austerity package [appreciation, -reaction] that has followed. (09 - 10 - 2012)

Extract 5. 4. 4 (*BBC World News*)

It's **a controversial choice** [appreciation, -composition] though for some given tensions [affect, -security] of closer political and economic union and **the protests** [affect, -security] around Europe at the **desperate** [affect, -security] austerity measures being imposed on some countries [judgement, -propriety] in the Eurozone. (12 - 10 - 2012)

Within the BBC data, austerity was tracked in communications with topical contexts regarding the words *demonstrators* (Ex. 5. 4. 1), *demonstrations* (Ex. 5. 4. 2), *angry people* (Ex. 5. 4. 3), and *protest* (Ex. 5. 4. 4). These words projected responses concerning the effectiveness of the austerity measures. Such responses are evidenced in such expressions as 'it attempts to push through the tough austerity measures to cut its deficit' (Extract 5.4.1), 'austerity has been controversial that led to thousands of demonstrations' (Extract 5.4.2), 'the people angry about the austerity package' (Extract 5.4.3) and 'the protests around Europe at the desperate austerity measures' (Extract 5.4.4) and so on. Austerity was evaluated through the negative meanings carried in the collocations of words such as *tough*, *controversial*, *angry about*, and *desperate*. Along with a series of such collocates, austerity was contextualised in a negative response of the affected. However, agency, the governments, and the pusher of austerity or austerity measures were highlighted less in the discourse. This indicated the BBC's attitude concerning the issue of the Eurozone Crisis, which was oriented to the reactions of ordinary people rather than to governmental responses in the tension of austerity. Thus, the BBC focused on emotive responses of the ordinary people aroused by the austerity measures.

In the discourse from CCTV, austerity, with its collocations of *measures*, *package*, and so forth, occurred mostly as a working issue under official discussion, as shown in the following examples.

Extract 5.4.5 (*CCTV News Update*)

The new figures have some asking [affect, +inclination] if austerity is to **blame** [judgement,-veracity] as Jack Barton reports. (02 – 10 – 2012)

Extract 5.4.6 (*CCTV News Update*)

Representatives of Greece's creditors have left the office of Greek Prime Minister Antonis Samaras after more talks on the details of a two year austerity package [appreciation,-composition,neutral]. (02 – 10 – 2012)

Extract 5.4.7 (*CCTV News Update*)

Greece is expected [judgement, +propriety] to announce **painful budget cuts** [appreciation,-reaction] soon to **satisfy** [affect, + satisfaction] international lenders and the government will unveil **a tough austerity budget** [appreciation,-reaction] later on [Monday, after its finance minister concludes a meeting with the International Monetary Fund, the European Commission and European Central Bank inspectors]. (02 – 10 – 2012)

Extract 5.4.8 (*CCTV News Update*)

Hopes of a deal [affect, + inclination/ appreciation, + composition] between the Greek government and the troika on austerity measures [appreciation,-composition] ahead of the meeting of euro zone finance ministers were **dashed** [judgement, -capability] on Saturday. (07 – 10 – 2012)

Extract 5.4.9 (*CCTV News Update*)

Over in Greece, now Greek Finance Minister Yannis Stournaras has held talks on austerity measures [appreciation, -composition] with representatives of the troika, that is, the European Commission, International Monetary Fund and European Central Bank. (14 – 10 – 2012)

Extract 5.4.10 (*CCTV News Update*)

Um over to where **the trouble** [appreciation, -reaction] is over in Europe, thousands of people gathered in Madrid on Saturday to voice **their anger** [affect, -happiness] at austerity measures [appreciation, -composition] introduced by the Spanish government. (14 – 10 – 2012)

Extract 5.4.11 (*CCTV News Update*)

In Europe, Portugal's government has announced **its toughest budget** [appreciation, -reaction] yet for next year, taking the bailed-out country deeper into austerity [appreciation, -reaction]. (16 – 10 – 2012)

Extract 5. 4. 12 (*CCTV News Update*)

While European leaders are in Brussels trying to **tackle Europe's financial woes** [judgement, + propriety], thousands of Greeks impacted by past EU decisions [judgement,-normality], is taking to the streets for another anti-austerity demonstration [judgement,-propriety]. (18 – 10 – 2012)

Extract 5. 4. 13 (*CCTV News Update*)

And over to Greece, around 70, 000 protesters [judgement,-propriety] have taken to the streets of Athens, in two separate demonstrations against austerity cutbacks [judgement,-propriety]. (18 – 10 – 2012)

In most of the examples above, austerity is also projected as a negative decision made by governments to tackle the Euro Crisis (Exs. 5. 4. 6 – 9, 10 – 12), and the word appeared along with such phrases as *if austerity to blame*, *toughest budget*, *painful budget cuts*, *tackle Europe's financial woes* and so on. These expressions indicate European states' efforts to push austerity measures. Thus, different from the treatment of austerity by the BBC as the subject entity that results in the negative responses of the ordinary people, austerity in the CCTV texts became the target or the topical object for the European leaders to push. The themes of these utterances were involved with the messages voiced from the 'government of EU members" (Exs. 5.4.6 – 9, 11, and 12) and from 'EU institutions (Troika)'. Only in Extracts 6 and 9 was the voice of the protesters reported. This reflected CCTV's attitude that favours the framing of the austerity issue in connection with its pusher, the agency of the austerity measures.

In short, analysis of the semantics of the contextual collocations revealed that the agency and the affected in the discourse of austerity were projected differently in BBC and CCTV representations. In the BBC news, if austerity resulted in a build-up of tension between the ordinary people and the government, austerity was exposed, along with its consequences, which resulted in the popular responses of the people being described with words such as *angry*, *demonstrations*, *protests*, *desperate*, and so forth. In the CCTV news, austerity was framed in a series of official or governmental endeavours aimed at implementing the austerity measures.

The standing of the news was also reflected through the preferences in representation. The interest of ordinary people as the affected seemed to be the favoured news discourse in BBC coverage; the attention at CCTV was the fulfilment of austerity measures, intensifying austerity as an official operation.

5.5 Conclusions

This comparative analysis first concerned the distribution of attitudinal resources in the discourse of TV news presentations at BBC and CCTV. The findings revealed that although no big divergences existed among the choices of attitudinal resources between the two organizations, some differences were perceived in other regards. For instance, the slight difference in the survey of binary attitudes resulted in suggesting that the CCTV held a somewhat positive attitude to some themes of the event such as ECB and IMF's efforts to bailout fund and the BBC holding a negative attitude to the impact of austerity measures.

This difference resulted in the further examination of the distribution of the subcategories of the resources. This analysis indicated a tendency on the part of CCTV to be more involved with **inclination**. The BBC seemed to care more about **security** in the domain of affect. The CCTV focused on the Eurozone Crisis in terms of the proposed austerity package as policy-making inclined by the Euro governments; the BBC focused on the ordinary people's responses and the consequences of austerity measures planned by the official summit. The CCTV made judgements in line with **tenacity** and

propriety; the BBC preferred **propriety** and **normality. Appreciation** in the CCTV data set was usually oriented to the dimension of **reaction**; in the BBC data, this resource concerned how things are composed. Thus, the detailed analysis of **attitude** was helpful in mapping the linguistic deployment of news texts to communicate social meanings.

Findings concerning the exploration of the linguistic mechanism of attribution employed in the BBC and the CCTV news discourse revealed that the BBC exploited attribution as a strategic device less than the CCTV. However, based on the distinction between attribution and the utterance averred, the patterns of attribution occurring in the CCTV and BBC data sets resulted in distinguishing averral-like statements from attributions in terms of epistemological positioning. Along with this line, the BBC seemed to prefer using averral-like statements. Such statements instilled more subjectivity into the news discourse, characterized with the communicative function of proclaiming rather than attributing and with being dialogically contractive rather than expansive. In contrast, the CCTV preferred attribution, although some averral-like statements were also identified. This indicated that CCTV news used attribution to constrain subjectivity, making the discourse more dialogically expansive.

Finally, the discourse of austerity was explored to identify how the agency and the affected were discursively represented in the BBC and CCTV data sets. The semantic prosody of austerity revealed that the BBC employed austerity prominently, from a populist perspective, with the collocations about affectedness (i. e., the ordinary people's responses) to reinforce the consequences that austerity measures evoked. The CCTV situated austerity with collocations about agency, foregrounding austerity as the object of official or governmental endeavours being pushed. These contrasting perspectives in representing austerity also indicated the different attitudes held by the CCTV and BBC concerning the participants as news topicality in the context of the Eurozone Crisis.

In summary, the BBC and CCTV shared much in terms of their attitudinal stance towards to the Eurozone Crisis; the data revealed some significant differences. The use of attitudinal resources tended to be similar in the distribution of both the attitude resources and polarity of attitude. One of the salient differences was generally attributed to the intersubjective stance taken by both institutions and other ideologies discursively represented with reference to the austerity. In other words, the CCTV tended be dialogically expansive by attributing the news utterance; whereas the BBC was likely to adopt averral-like statements to diminish a dialogic possibility.

Another difference lay in the representation of 'austerity' in the Euro Crisis. The CCTV focused on the Euro governments as pusher of austerity measures; instead, the BBC was more concerned about the emotive responses of the affected people.

Chapter 6 Realizations of Stance in the Television News Coverage of the Boston Bombing: A Comparative Study of CCTV and BBC Television News Presentations

6.1 A General Description of the Data

A bombing took place during the U. S. Boston Marathon on 15 April 2013, killing 3 people and injuring an estimated 264 others. This event was soon covered by many of the major broadcasters, including the BBC and the CCTV. The bombing during the Boston Marathon had some news value for these broadcasters for it deviated from the routine events, which was an unusual and unexpected with negative social impacts. Its negative nature interacts with 'unexpectedness' (Montgomery 2007:8), which became the headline news for the BBC and the CCTV.

This case study was based on the data collected from the CCTV and the BBC news presentations from 16 April 2013 to the end of April 2013. The presenters' discourses were transcribed into written form. The CCTV transcripts consisted of 27 fragments with a total of 1,316 words; the BBC data consisted of 19 extracts with a total of 1,575 words.

6.2 Attitude as Realization of Stance in the Television News Coverage of the Boston Bombing

Based upon appraisal theory (Martin & White, 2005), coding of both the CCTV and BBC news texts involved the application of the subsystems in **attitude** (**affect**, **judgement** and **appreciation**). **Affect** deals with emotions and feelings. For example, words such as *shocked* and *ashamed* in the locution of 'his family are shocked and ashamed by what his nephews did' were explicit realizations of affect. **Judgement** deals with evaluation of people and people's behaviours. For example, 'Boston Marathon bombings' was invoked as a negative activity against moral norms in people's lives and that should be condemned; the phrase 'working around the clock' in the utterance 'police was said to be working around the clock' was also implicitly appraised as positive **judgement** of police performance in working hard to investigate the bombing. **Appreciation** deals with things or phenomena. For example, the Boston Marathon was framed as 'one of the world's great sporting events' in the context of the sentence 'these explosions have cast a long shadow over one of the world's great sporting events'. As such it was the realisation of attitude in terms of appreciation.

Attitude as realization of stance has been addressed in this chapter to compare how CCTV and the BBC made attitudinal choices. The chapter also contains an examination of the explicit and implicit realization of **attitude** in the news coverage of the Boston bombing.

6.2.1 A Comparative Investigation into Attitude in the CCTV and BBC Television News Coverage of the Boston Bombing

This section compares how **attitude** operates in the discourse of the Boston bombing across the two news institutions. The comparison consists of two steps. The first step was an examination of the distribution of **affect**, **judgement**, and **appreciation** in both news data sets to find similarities and differences in the news representations of the two news organizations in a general sense. The second step was to examine the polarity of the attitudinal choices in the news texts to determine what dimensions of **attitude** (i. e. , the subcategories of each attitudinal category; positive or negative) each news institution held with regard to the event.

Table 18 shows the global distribution of each **attitude** category in the news texts of the CCTV and the BBC.

Table 18 Comparison of Attitude Resource Distribution

Resources	*CCTV News Update*		*BBC World News*	
	f	%	*f*	%
Affect	15	14. 85	25	20. 16
Judgement	54	53. 47	65	52. 42
Appreciation	32	31. 68	34	27. 42
Totals	101	100. 00	134	100. 00

The comparative survey showed both similarities and differences in the adoption of the three categories of attitude. For example, both news organizations attached importance to judgement, the orientation of subjectivity or attitude to the people and their behaviours. **Judgement** in both news texts exceeded other resources (53. 47% in the CCTV data; 52. 42% in the BBC data). Both data sets also revealed equal treatment in the evaluation of things or processes. **Appreciation** was the secondary resource exploited by both news texts (31. 68% in the CCTV data;27. 42% in the BBC data). **Affect**, although the least used resource in both data sets, was different between the two organizations in proportion of use. The rate of its use for the BBC was 20. 16%, and for CCTV was 14. 85%. These results indicate although the BBC and the CCTV have been similar in adopting **judgement** as the leading attitudinal choice, the CCTV has tended to adopt

appreciation more than the BBC and the BBC has tended to use **affect** more than CCTV.

Table 19 shows the distribution of the subcategories of attitudinal resources revealed in both data sets.

Table 19 Comparison of Distribution of Attitudinal Resource Subcategories

Resource subcategory	*CCTV News Update*		*BBC World News*	
	f	%	*f*	%
Affect				
● Security	5	4.95	10	8.06
● Satisfaction	1	0.99	0	0.00
● Inclination	4	3.96	2	1.61
● Happiness	5	4.95	13	10.48
Judgement				
● Normality	5	4.95	9	7.26
● Capacity	0	0.00	2	1.61
● Tenacity	8	7.92	7	5.65
● Veracity	2	1.98	4	3.23
● Propriety	39	38.61	43	34.67
Appreciation				
● Reaction	18	17.82	20	16.13
● Composition	3	2.97	6	4.84
● Valuation	11	10.89	8	6.45
Totals	101	100.00	124	100.00

Table 20 Comparison of Attitudinal Polarity

Resource subcategory	*CCTV News Update*				*BBC World News*			
	Positive		Negative		Positive		Negative	
	f	%	*f*	%	*f*	%	*f*	%
Affect								
● Security	0	0.00	5	4.95	1	0.80	9	7.26
● Satisfaction	0	0.00	1	0.99	0	0.00	0	0.00
● Inclination	4	3.96	0	0.00	2	1.61	0	0.00
● Happiness	0	0.00	5	4.95	1	0.80	12	9.68
Judgement								
● Normality	2	1.98	3	2.97	4	3.23	5	4.03
● Capacity	0	0.00	0	0.00	0	0.00	2	1.61
● Tenacity	8	7.92	0	0.00	5	4.03	2	1.61
● Veracity	2	1.98	0	0.00	3	2.42	1	0.80
● Propriety	11	10.89	28	27.72	9	7.26	34	27.42
Appreciation								
● Reaction	0	0.00	18	17.82	5	4.03	15	12.10
● Composition	0	0.00	3	2.97	0	0.00	6	4.84
● Valuation	3	2.97	8	7.92	3	2.42	5	4.03
Totals	30	36.96	71	63.04	33	26.60	91	73.40

Table 20 shows the distribution of the polarity of attitudinal choices, by subcategory, across both data sets. Both the CCTV and the BBC showed a striking resemblance in the binary distribution of attitudes. Well over half of all the attitudinal resources in each organization were deemed to evoke negative responses after the Boston bombing occurred. Negative attitude was 63.04% in the CCTV data and 73.40% in the BBC data, results that are hardly surprising because this similarity may be attributed to the nature of the event. That is, the attitudes represented in the news coverage of this event are similarly negative because the Boston bombing itself was thematically anti-humanity in nature, so the similar attitudes held by the CCTV and the BBC coincide with the notion of journalistic 'sphere of consensus' (Hallin, 1984: 21, 1986: 117). The *sphere of consensus* is the journalistic 'region of motherhood and apple pie', in which 'journalists do not feel compelled to present opposing views, and indeed often feel it their responsibility to act as advocates or ceremonial protectors of consensus values' (1984: 21). Therefore, in this case, both the BBC and the CCTV arrived at a general consensus concerning the Boston bombing by projecting its negative effect, because the bombing as a terror act was against the morals of the normal social orders, that is, not socially acceptable for both news institutions.

Similarly, **judgement** was the main choice of attitudinal expression for both the CCTV and the BBC. The subcategory of **propriety** was the most prominent resource (38.61% in CCTV coverage; 34.67% in BBC coverage). This suggested that people and their behaviours tended to be subject to negative evaluation in the dimension of ethics and legal morals. A critical treatment used by both the CCTV and the BBC was the description of the evaluated targets, the bombing and people's behaviour, as a crime, a terrorist attack, or a conspiracy. Formulations such as 'those responsible for this act', 'suspect', 'bomb attacks', '[people] using a weapon of mass destruction to kill people', and '[the men they described as] armed and dangerous' were explicitly inscribed in the texts. Thus, the actions were coded as negative **propriety** because the semantics were associated with wrong deeds against normative social morals; thus, they should be criticised.

Affect was relatively under-used by the BBC (20.15%) and CCTV (14.85%) (see Table 19) in comparison with other attitudinal choices. Indeed, the BBC news expressed **affect** from the threads of **security** and **happiness**, a kind of mental process directing personal emotions at an external trigger or environment. **Happiness** deals with some negative formulations such as 'sympathies', 'condolences', 'dealing with the aftermath', and 'are with all those who have been affected'. Such emotive revelations project the emotional responses to the event by some participants negatively. Differing slightly from this scenario, CCTV expressed **affect** from the angles of negative **security** and positive **inclination**.

In particular, positive **inclination** reflected a strong desiderative rather than an emotive mental process. For example, 'ask for' showed a strong but positive wish in the following example: 'The FBI has released photos and video images of two suspects in the Boston Marathon bombings and is asking for [affect, + inclination] the public's help in identifying them' (CCTV news, 19 – 04 – 2013). Thus, words such as *hail* (the police response), *request*, *stresses*, and *believe* suggested that some participants were much positively engaged with the investigation of this event. Finally, the treatment of **appreciation** across both news texts was not divergent in their dealing with things, processes, and so forth from the dimensions of **reaction**, **composition**, and **valuation**.

6.2.2 Inscribed and Invoked Attitude

Along with the elaborations identified in Martin & White (2005), indirect realizations of **attitude** may include ideational material that invokes attitudes by direct inscriptions. One key to understanding this involves contextual prosody that may direct viewers to an attitudinal reading of the text. For instance, the word *explosion* may be considered a non-attitudinal lexis without context. In the context of the Boston Marathon Bombing, the word may be appreciated as a negative happening. Martin & White (2005) suggested that as the text unfolds, 'inscribed attitude, in other words, launches and subsequently reinforces a prosody which direct readers in their evaluation of non-attitudinal ideational material under its scope' (p. 64). In this sense, contextual prosody has an important part in colouring its local texts. Understanding of this should be helpful, in particular, when appraising an **attitude** invoked in hard-news texts, as seen in the case analysis of the Syria Crisis. Similarly, in the present case, both the CCTV and the BBC appeared to be involved with invocations, that is, the invoking of some attitudinal meanings through contextual prosody. The most obvious instance involved factual formulations, such as 'two people have died' and 'twenty eight people are injured', which invoked an attitudinal response when they worked together with 'two bomb devices went off' near the finish line of the Boston Marathon race. The factual and non-attitudinal wordings were coloured in this context and could be interpreted to express a sympathetic sentiment to the affected and a **judgement** of condemnation over the act of bombing.

Moreover, beyond the semantic workings of lexical formulations, a diversity of indirect realizations of **attitude** was revealed in the BBC's discourse representation of the Boston bombing. This involved the use of rhetorical devices such as metaphor and other mechanisms that connoted or flagged attitude, as shown in the following extracts:

Extract 6.2.1 (description; *BBC World News*)

More now on that situation in Boston where the residents in Watertown are being told to stay indoors [affect, -security] as the hunt for one of the suspects [judgement, +propriety] in the Boston Marathon shooting [judgement, -propriety] continues. (19-04-2013)

Extract 6.2.2 (contrast and comparison; *BBC World News*)

A city that should be **celebrating**① [affect, +happiness] the end of its annual Marathon but instead dealing with [affect, -happiness] the aftermath [appreciation, -composition] of **the worst bombing** [appreciation, -reaction] on US soil since 9/11. (16-04-2013)

Extract 6.2.3 (metaphor; *BBC World News*)

He told me what it was like to be knocked to the ground [appreciation, -reaction] by the force of the blast [appreciation, -composition]. (16-04-2013)

---

① Note: The attitude inscribed are indicated by bold so as to be distinguished from the attitude invoked designated by the element underlined.

Extract 6.2.4 (exposition; BBC World News)

The bomb [judgement, -propriety] we were told contained nails, ball bearings [appreciation, -composition] and was possibly inside a pressure cooker [appreciation, -composition]. (17-04-2013)

Extract 6.2.5 (quotation and empathy; *BBC World News*)

British Prime Minister David Cameron released a statement [judgement, + tenacity] saying the scenes from Boston are **shocking** [affect, -security]. That's a quote from him. "My thoughts," he says, "are with all those who have been affected [affect, -happiness]." (16-04-2013)

Although these extracts contained a range of mechanisms to provoke or invite attitude, the formulation in each example was different in its loading of rhetorical property. For example, in Extract 6.2.1, a '[that] situation' is evaluated through a piece of description 'where the residents in Watertown are being told to stay indoors'. This description, which contains a reference to the context of 'explosion in Boston Marathon' under which the 'hunt for one of the suspects' is continuing could necessarily provoke an attitude of insecurity concerning the situation. In Extract 6.2.2, although the phrase *deal with* could be non-attitudinal out of this context, through the adversative connective *but* and the adjunct *instead*, which contrasts with the positively **inscribed attitude** *celebrating*, then *deal with* was negatively invoked. At the same time, the aftermath of the Boston bombing (*the worst bombing on U. S. soil since* 9/11) was compared 'as bad as' the 9/11 event, maintaining and reinforcing the degree of negative invocation.

Attitude was also invoked through other rhetorical devices, including metaphor (Ex. 6. 2. 3), an expository account of bomb making (Ex. 6. 2. 4), and quoted expressions of empathy such as 'my thoughts are with all those who have been affected' (Ex. 6. 2. 5). Because associative emotions or attitudes could be aroused by the use of ideational materials, these additional rhetorical mechanisms were employed to intensify the speaker's affectual disposition.

In short, some similarities exist in terms of attitudinal stance realised in the news coverage of the Boston bombing between the CCTV and the BBC. First, both the CCTV and the BBC projected the event as negative by adopting negative attitudinal choices more than positive ones. Most of the negative attitudinal choices were focused on the judgements of the suspects and their behaviours, which were morally unacceptable. Second, the CCTV and the BBC used similar methods to indirectly realiaze attitude, invoking attitudes via contextual connotations. However, some differences can also be noted. Apart from **judgement** adopted, the CCTV tended to use **appreciation** more than **affect**; whereas the BBC showed a tendency towards **affect** more than **appreciation**. In addition, the BBC realized attitudinal invocations through the rhetorical mechanisms of metaphors, comparison and contrast, expository accounts, and quotations of empathy to arouse their viewers' associative meanings.

6.3 Attribution as Realization of Stance

Stance can be realized through attribution in news discourse. News presenters accomplish this through their choice of reporting verbs and sayers, the social identities of source descriptors, the evaluative potentials of the attributed statements, and the forms of attribution they employ.

Table 21 shows the results of the survey of reporting words used by the CCTV and the BBC in their coverage of the Boston bombing. The ratios for *say* (*say* plus *said*) were 70% (35% plus 35%) in the CCTV data set and 81.81% (36.36% plus 45.45%) in the BBC data set. This reporting verb was the most chosen method for achieving stance through attribution, suggesting that the structure of 'X says/said Y' was prominent in both CCTV and the BBC news coverage. A selection of instances of *say/said* have been reported in Table 21, which shows that although CCTV employed diverse reporting words, such as *according to* and *confirm*, both the CCTV and the BBC seemed to rely on *say* or *said* to formulate news propositions that maintained a neutral position.

Table 21　Reporting Words Employed in News Coverage of the Boston Bombing

Reporting words/verbs	CCTV News Update		BBC World News	
	f	%	*f*	%
Say	7	35.00	4	36.36
Said	7	35.00	5	45.45
According to	2	10.00	0	0.00
Confirm	3	15.00	1	9.09
Stress	1	5.00	0	0.00
Announce	0	0.00	1	9.09
Totals	20	100.00	11	100.00

In a general sense, attribution in the case of the Boston bombing was concerned with the common and usual use of *X say* or *X said*, which is employed to construe the authorial voice as neutral or to achieve a minimization of the writers' responsibility for the attributed material. However, the CCTV and the BBC varied in the practice of attribution exercised by journalists and the sources attributed, along with attributed propositions in attributions, which might be related to the respective norms or conventions of news making, especially with regard to evidentiality. The nature of the source provides the evidential standing, which positions the viewers to see the propositions attributed as true, credible, or warrantable (White, 2006). In this case, the *sayers* in the instances of *say/said* in the CCTV and the BBC news were identified as five categories of voice (Table 22): law enforcement; government, including those of the United States and other foreign states; hospitals; civilians, including the suspects and victims; with a residual category for unspecified.

Table 22 Categorisation of Sayer in News Coverage of the Boston Bombing

Category	CCTV News Update			BBC World News		
	f	%	Instance	*f*	%	Instance
Law enforcement	7	41.18	Intelligence officials; the U. S. federal source; a person briefed on the investigation.	3	33.33	The FBI; the investigators; police
Government (US and other)	3	17.65	The president; a White House official; U. S. President Barack Obama	5	55.56	British Prime Minister David Cameron; Afganistan Hamid Karzai; Julia Gillard; President Obama; the White House

（续上表）

Category	CCTV News Update			BBC World News		
	f	%	Instance	*f*	%	Instance
Hospital	1	5.88	Hospital officials	0	0.00	
Civilians (including suspects and victims)	4	23.53	The father of the two men suspected; the suspects' uncle, Ruslan Tsarni;	0	0.00	
Unspecified	2	11.76	The source; the killed suspect is said	1	11.11	His condition is said
Total	17	100.00		9	100.00	

As shown in Table 22, the accessed voices in the CCTV news coverage included all five categories, a wider range of voices than used in the BBC coverage. Most of the voices in the CCTV coverage were categorized as law enforcement (41.18%); whereas in the BBC data, most of the voices were categorized as government (55.56%). Both news organizations did not specify some sources. However, CCTV chose to use voices from the categories of hospitals and civilians; whereas the BBC did not do so.

Multiple voices adopted in the news indicated that the news was sourced from different perspectives. However, different choices in news sources also revealed journalistic preference for one source or another. The CCTV used more sources from law enforcement, such as the FBI and police officials, which resulted in positioning the audience to view their propositional content as reliable and warrantable. On the other hand, because the voices of *sayer* play a constructive role in the knowledge of news, CCTV news, which drew upon voices from the investigating institutions, seemed to employ an investigative style of news reporting for this event. The audience was informed of progress in the investigation from the voice of law enforcement, thus creating the expectation that law enforcement account for the Boston Bombing. Attributed materials that consisted of the factual elements involved with the case under investigation were relatively less affective. *Sayer* in the BBC data was more involved with the voice of government officials, highlighting the role of government in the news coverage of the event.

Among the nine formulations of *X say/said Y* in the BBC data, three worked intensively in informing the condolences extended to the victims from the internationally-known political figures identified in the same news items. These condolences were buried in the neutral use of *say*, as shown in the following extract:

Extract 6.3.1 (*BBC World News*)

> British Prime Minister David Cameron released a statement saying the scenes from Boston are shocking. That's a quote from him. "My thoughts," he says, "are with all those who have been affected."

> Julia Gillard, the Australian prime minister said our condolences go to the families of those killed. —And the president of Afganistan Hamid Karzai sent his condolences while saying: "Having suffered from terrorist attacks, our people feel better the pain and suffering arising from such incidents." (16 –04 –2013)

The attributed propositions were statements of condolences that carried heavily sympathetic voices and attitudes toward the people killed. However, the authorial neutral standing was inflicted with the attitudinal potentials of the attributed proposition, possibly arousing an emotional evaluation. On one hand, the expression of condolences was formative in BBC news knowledge; on the other hand, its use of these expressions instilled an affective element in the news reporting of the Boston Bombing.

Attributions were also realized in other forms in the BBC news. ' We heard/learned from the source or we are told' appeared different from the traditional use of *X say/said Y*, which was widely adopted in the CCTV coverage. In the terms of evidential standing, CCTV usually distanced an authorial voice by employing the reporting words as a device of attribution; the reporting words expressed indirect evidence that the propositions might be based on hearsay. However, the BBC attached more authorial engagement (the use of the first person *we*) to build up news knowledge through ways other than attribution, using the pronoun *we* in attribution to base the propositional contents on direct witness evidence or perception, thus indicating that propositions did not need more evidence, as shown in Extract 6.3.2.

Extract 6.3.2 (*BBC World News*)

We have learned from the White House the president will be going up to Boston for what's been called an interfaith service on Thursday in memorial of those who were attacked at the Marathon. **We**'ve also heard from the FBI that they have recovered what they think are fragments of a black nylon bag that was used to hold the bomb. The bomb we were told contained nails, ball bearings and was possibly inside a pressure cooker. (17-04-2013)

In Extract 6.3.2, attributed propositions were based on 'our' first-hand evidence suggested by the use of *we* (in bold). By attributing propositions in this way, the BBC positioned the audience to view these attributed propositions as trustworthy and warrantable because the external source (i.e., the White House or FBI) segues into first-hand evidence through the use of *we*. Thus, *we* was turned into a main source of the propositions attributed, overriding the real source. The news knowledge of the event was constructed in an authorial-acknowledging voice in contrast with CCTV's usual use of reporting words and was presented through many different external voices.

Sometimes, first-hand evidence was directly presented with no attribution to any external source, as is shown in Extract 6.3.3:

Extract 6.3.3 (*BBC World News*)

> Now we bring you some breaking news from Boston where police gunfire has apparently been heard on the police scanner. (09-04-2013)

In this case, *we* was identified as the source of the proposition, indicating first-hand evidence. *Apparently* indicated the basis of the journalist's knowledge lay 'in "obviousness" or "self-evidence" of what is modified' (Bednarek, 2006 b, p. 641). The use of we in the BBC data set also served to base the news propositions between known and unknown. Usually, *we* as the news source reported what news knowledge had been acquired. Sometimes, however, it reported what had not been acquired, as shown in the following extracts:

Extracts 6.3.4 (*BBC World News*)

> I know around this time information **gets a bit thin**, but

what can you tell us? (16 –04 –2013)

Extracts 6.3.5 (*BBC World News*)

But a day later, we still **don't know** who carried out these attacks or why. (17 –04 –2013)

Extracts 6.3.6 (*BBC World News*)

What is still not known when a specially trained team of investigators will be able to question the teenaged suspect, Dzhokhar Tsarnaev, which is under guard in hospital with a gunshot injury to the throat? (23 –04 –2013)

Applying unknown knowledge to the news report could have the effect of impressing the audience with journalistic alignment in seeking the truth of the event. It also stressed on-the-spot reporting and the immediacy of the news. In a global sense, *BBC World News* interplayed known and unknown knowledge, the tension from which served to identify journalistic authority as that of a first-hand witness. Thus, BBC tried to synchronise investigative truth with its news sources.

CCTV news differed in the use of reporting words, attributing more propositions to the *sayer* as law enforcement. Doing so resulted in projecting the progress of the case under investigation. The BBC instilled affective elements into the investigative event by adopting condolences extended from government officials. The BBC also realized attribution by embedding journalistic voice as investigating the case rather than having investigated it. This shift in dealing with reporting perspectives resulted in the event being projected as CCTV's report on the investigation into the Boston bombing. The BBC also made the reporting of the event seem as if it were investigating the case.

6.4 Agency and Affectedness: Suspects in News Representation

van Leeuwen (1996) suggested two different understandings of agency. One is the sociological concept of agency, an important concept in critical discourse analysis, 'which means in which context which social actors are represented as "agents" and which as "patients"' (van Leeuwen, 1996, p. 32). The other is the grammatical concept of agency found in Halliday (1994). However, he also argued that sociological agency is not always realized by the grammatical role of agent and that no neat fit exists between sociological and linguistic categories in investigating the representation of agency. In this dissertation, the two concepts of agency and affectedness were addressed from a discourse perspective to examine CCTV and BBC representation of these concepts in the event structure of the Boston bombing, thus going beyond Hallidayan lexico-grammatical speculation. The notions of agency and affectedness on the discourse level could be seen in the event of the Boston bombing as who volitionally initiated the act of bombing and who was affected from the bombs. This analysis was conducted because the running news coverage of the event was developmental in temporal and topical evolution; thus, the social participants were not necessarily invariant in the two different institutionalised discourse representations. However, agency remained relatively stable in holding responsibility for the event despite whoever participated in successive news reports. Thus questions were raised concerning how agency and the affected were evaluatively positioned and whether the relevant social bonds between social participants resulted in sentiments over agency and affectedness in television news presentation.

With bombing as a key concept of action in news coverage, agency in the investigative discourse of the Boston bombing was designated as the suspects being sought. These suspects were finally identified as two brothers, Dzohkhar Tsarnaev and Tamerlan Tsarnaev. The victims were the patients directly affected by causative connection with the bombing attack by the suspects. However, the discursive representation of the suspects or the victims in the continuous news coverage of CCTV and BBC contained both similarities and variations in their choices concerning the participant as social actor. First of all, the suspects were identified on 18 April 2013, two days after the bombing event. As shown in Extracts 6.4.1 and 6.4.2, news presenters described them as 'brothers' and as teenaged, 'nice', and 'ordinary' school boys:

Extract 6.4.1 (*BBC World News*)

> And we'll be addressing that motive in just a second, but let's get a little bit more now on these suspects. As we've been reporting, they were brothers-Tamerlan Tsarnaev attended a public high school in Cambridge, Massachusetts and he was at school there. We've been hearing that they were nice, ordinary boys. Laura Trevelyan up there in Boston, what've you been hearing about the suspects and what they were like. (20-04-2013)

Extract 6.4.2 (*CCTV News Update*)

> The two suspects in the bombings are brothers, believed to be from Dagestan in Russia. Reports coming in from Boston say that the suspect who was killed was the older of the two. The killed suspect [is said to have been studying to be an engineer at the Bunker Hill Community College in Boston, Massachusetts.] (20-04-2013)

However, these ordinary people seemed to be extraordinary

in contrast with their behavioural engagement with the bombing attack. Indeed, from a journalistic point of view, although a factual element covered in the news report, it resulted in drawing the audience's attention to the suspects' motives for the bombing.

Second, because the news coverage of the event was evolving in micro-topics and timeline, juxtaposition of participants as social actors in factual reporting might have indicated journalistic attitude and invoked sentiments in a given context. In general, the coparticipants in news reporting about the suspects appeared to be variously involved with the FBI, the public, police, the prosecutor, security officials, journalists, and even relatives of the suspects. The co-occurrence of the social actors in tracking the suspects included FBI, the public, police, the prosecutor, and security officials, indicating an inferential connection that the suspects should be legally punished.

However, CCTV and BBC news presenters varied in identification of the other social actors co-occurring in the factual reporting of the suspects. The factual reporting of the suspects through description could have given to other possible interpretations of **judgement** of the suspect. For example, in the BBC data, suspects were reported as fighting with the police resulting in one being killed and one surviving, as shown in Extracts 6.4.3 and 6.4.4:

Extracts 6. 4. 3 (*BBC World News*)

Now the surviving suspect who is still in hospital in serious condition, has been charged with conspiring to use a weapon of mass destruction. (23 –04 –2013)

Extracts 6. 4. 4 (*BBC World News*)

And US security officials are to face questions in congress over whether they mishandled the information about the Boston Bombings suspect, Tamerlan Tsarnaev. (24 –04 –2013)

In the first case, the BBC's journalistic description suggested somewhat humanistic sympathy over the surviving suspect who was injured in fighting with the police although he was charged for his involvement with the bombing. In the second case, through the factual reporting of Congress questioning security officials over whether they mishandled the case of the killed suspect, the BBC acknowledged Congress's authority to question the security officials and thus stayed away from legal sanctions against the suspects.

In the CCTV news data, identification of the other social actors in reporting the suspects also resulted in different interpretations of *suspect*, as shown in the following extract:

Extract 6.4.5 (*CCTV News Update*)

According to doctors, 11 people are still in the hospital. Three are in serious condition. Earlier, Boston's police commissioner said the Boston Marathon bombing suspects had likely been planning other attacks. (23 – 04 – 2013)

Here, coparticipants (i. e., doctors and victims) were juxtaposed with suspects in this context. In contrast with the three victims hospitalised for their serious conditions, the subjunctive utterance of preplanning other attacks resulted in a severe condemnation of the suspects.

Alternative voices were also expressed through the relatives of the suspects, as shown in Extracts 6.4.6 and 6.4.7:

Extract 6.4.6 (*CCTV News Update*)

The suspects' uncle, Ruslan Tsarni, says his family are shocked and ashamed by what his nephews did. He also stresses that his family has nothing to do with them. He said the suspects "being losers" drove them to commit this tragedy. (20 – 04 – 2013)

Extract 6.4.7 (*CCTV News Update*)

The aunt and uncle of the Boston bombing suspects have spoken to the media, expressing their disbelief that the two brothers could have committed the attacks. (23 – 04 – 2013)

The CCTV adopted voices from the suspects' relatives to express their sentiments and attitudes to the bombing event as well as to explicitly evaluate the suspects as 'being losers'. These expressions seemed to strengthen the standpoint that what the suspects did went beyond the base line of family kindness and could not be forgiven even by their family members. Such uses of the relatives' voices continued to define the nature of bombing, along with moral condemnation.

Compared to the representation of agency in news coverage, the victims identified as directly affected were less covered in both the BBC and the CCTV news discourse. Although both organizations reported the number of victims affected in the bombing, CCTV also employed some ways to draw the audience's attention to the affected. For example, CCTV included placed more details about the identification of the victims, such as one of the victims being a 'Chinese national', which evoked emotional consonance among Chinese audiences:

Extract 6.4.8 (*CCTV News Update*)

> The third person killed in the Boston Marathon blasts has been identified as a Chinese national. This was confirmed [by officials from the Chinese Consulate General in New York. Relatives have requested anonymity for the deceased.] (17 – 04 – 2013)

Another example was the reporting of the health situation of the victims hospitalised:

Extract 6.4.9 (*CCTV News Update*)

> Of the over 180 people being treated at hospitals, at least 17 are in critical condition and 41 are in serious condition. As of Tuesday afternoon, at least 51 have gone home. Hospital officials say many victims suffered injuries to the lower parts of their bodies. Boston Tufts Medical Center has cared for 14 victims, and all of them have shrapnel from the blasts. (17-04-2013)

CCTV supplied more detail about the medical treatment of the victims after the bombing. Verbal descriptions such as 'in critical condition', 'in serious condition', and 'suffered injuries to the lower parts of their bodies' reflected more sympathetic sentiments to those affected while also generating a tone of moral condemnation on the nature of the bombing act and its doers.

Thus, both CCTV and BBC reflected both agency and affectedness in their discursive projections. Both organizations positioned the suspects as agents responsible for the act of bombing through the factual description of the suspects and the juxtaposition of other social participants such as the FBI, police, and prosecutors. Both institutions contextualized the social identities of the co-participants in a legally investigative scenario.

However, CCTV seemed to go further and exerted moral criticism concerning the suspects by sourcing the voices of the suspect's relatives. Compared with their representation in agency, both news organizations did less in colouring the affectedness of the victims, reporting the number of casualties. CCTV achieved attachment to the victims by report details such as one of the victims who were killed being a Chinese national and the medical conditions of victims upon hospitalisation. Such representation results in drawing the audience's consonant sentiments to the victims and in enforcing a sense of condemnation for the suspects.

6.5 Conclusions

This analysis, based on White's (2006) framework, was an investigation of the linguistic mechanisms of attitude, attribution, agency and affectedness as realizations of stance in the CCTV and the BBC television news presentations. **Attitude** was investigated in terms of its subsystems (i. e., **affect**, **judgement**, and **appreciation**) as well as in terms of their distribution the attitudinal polarity in news coverage. In a general sense, both the CCTV and the BBC showed negative responses to the event, projecting the Boston bombing as a destructive event in normal social reality. This resemblance reflects some commonalities of journalistic norms shared by the CCTV and the BBC institutions, working in line with the notion of ‘sphere of consensus’, suggested by Hallin (1984; 1986). In terms of the attitudinal choices distributed in the news coverage, both news institutions attached the most importance to **judgement** rather than **affect** and **appreciation**, which indicated that the participants and their behaviours involved in this event were the focal point of evaluation. The evaluation in the dimension of **judgement** was oriented to **propriety**, the allocation of moral judgement and ethical values to the people involved, i. e., the suspects. However, each individual institution seemed to deal differently with **affect** and **appreciation**. The BBC had a tendency towards **affect** more than the CCTV; the CCTV was more engaged with **appreciation** than **affect**. The BBC's use of affect involved **security** and **happiness** and was imbued with negative tone. Thus, the BBC represented sentiments about safety and unhappiness about the event; whereas, the CCTV emphasised a positive **inclination** of **affect** to express a strong desire to call for action. In addition, **attitude** as realization of stance was inscribed and invoked on the level of expression. Attitudinal invocation was one of the characteristics found in the BBC news. Linguistic rhetorical devices, including description, exposition, metaphor, contrast and comparison, and empathy, served to position viewers to take an attitudinal orientation.

Attribution was also addressed in terms of the evaluative

potential of attribution. The BBC structured attributed propositions through attribution and its other forms of realization. The *sayer* as attributed source was identified and categorised into five voices: law enforcement, government, civilians, hospital and a category for unspecified. However, the distribution of the five voices was not the same in both news institutions. CCTV resorted to the voice of law enforcement; the BBC's voice was mainly that of government. The CCTV projected the event as an investigative case; the BBC, foregrounded the role of government to express condolences and affect. The BBC also explicitly embedded the journalistic voice by using the pronoun *we* to show authorial engagement with the event, specifically to base its news propositions on the play between known and unknown territories to strengthen the existence of witness's evidence of the event as reported.

Finally, based on a sociological rather than a grammatical understanding of agency, the representation of agency versus affectedness in the CCTV and BBC news coverage was examined. The designated agents of the suspects were positioned first through the factual reporting of their identities as 'ordinary' and 'nice' school boys, arousing questions about their motives for bombing. These agents were then evaluated as criminals deserving legal punishment through identification of the suspects under official investigation. The CCTV went even further, imposing moral criticism on the suspects through responses of being unbelievable and unforgivable to the suspects' relationship to their criminal deeds. Even though the CCTV represented affectedness less than agency, the CCTV placed more attachment to the victims in the hospital, which could result in invoking sympathy over the victims and exerting condemnation of the suspects.

The present study revealed the operation of stance by CCTV and the BBC in their television coverage of the Boston bombing. This finding was revealed through comparative analyses of attitude, attribution, agency, and affectedness. Attitudinally, the CCTV and the BBC held strikingly similar attitudes toward the event by adopting negative attitude choices, although there were subtleties in the verbal resources and language mechanisms used by the news broadcasters. Apart from the judgment adopted, the BBC tended to show more **affect** than did the CCTV; conversely, the CCTV was likely to show **appreciation** more than **affect**. In terms of examination of voices reported in attribution, the Boston bombing was depicted as an investigative case by the CCTV but as an event to be accounted for by the government by the BBC. The suspects and victims of the Boston bombing were also reported by both broadcasters. However, the CCTV went further to depict the suspects as criminals, arousing moral condemnation of them and sentiment for the victims.

Chapter 7 Realizations of Stance in the Television News Coverage of Typhoon Haiyan in the Philippines

7.1 A Description of the Data

Typhoon Haiyan, the deadliest tropical cyclone on record, made landfall in the Philippines on 8 November 2013, bringing devastation to Southeast Asia, especially the Philippines, where it resulted in over 6,000 deaths. Many broadcasters, including the CCTV and the BBC covered the typhoon. Television news presentations of Typhoon Haiyan on the CCTV and the BBC from 8 November 2013 to 26 November 2013 served as the data for this case study. Both the CCTV and the BBC television news presentation discourses were transcribed into written form. The CCTV data set included 41 news items with a total word count of 1,981; the BBC data set included 13 news items with a total word count of 1,286.

The event attracted the attention of many news broadcasters, such as the CCTV and the BBC, because the event was newsworthy in itself. First, Typhoon Haiyan brought damage and destruction to the Philippines and the negative nature of this event made it news. ' Bad news makes good news' (Montgomery, 2007, P. 8) and negativity is ' the basic news value' (Bell, 1991, P. 156). Second, Typhoon Haiyan appeared as headline news in the CCTV and the BBC news coverage partly because of its scale of huge impact, killing 6,000 people and bringing about devastating damage to the typhoon-stricken areas in the Philippines. Such ' events need to be of a scale large enough to warrant attention' (Montgomery, 2007, P. 6).

7.2 Attitude as Realization of Stance in the Television News Coverage of Typhoon Haiyan

The system of **attitude** from appraisal theory (Martin & White, 2005) served as the basis for coding both the CCTV and BBC news presentations. This coding enabled the examination of the realization of stance in both contexts.

7.2.1 Identification of Attitude

The three categories of attitudinal resources (i. e., **affect**, **judgement**, and **appreciation**) were identified in the discourses of the BBC and the CCTV. **Affect** deals with positive and negative responses in terms of feelings. In this case, lexis such as *warned* (affect, -security], *fear* (affect, -security), *causing people to* wonder (affect, + inclination), *anger* (affect, -happiness), and *frustration* (*affect*,-*satisfaction*) in the CCTV data set were coded as **affect** because of their emphasis on people's emotional responses. Similarly, the words such as *appealing for* (affect, + inclination) and *the misery* (affect,-happiness) were coded in the same way.

Judgement concerns attitude towards people and their behaviors, which one admires or criticizes, praises or condemns. In the CCTV texts, tokens such as 'vowed to handle the aftermath of the typhoon' (judgement, + tenacity) were coded **judgement** because of their orientation to people's behavior, which was dependable. Likewise, in the BBC texts, **judgement** was reflected through wordings such as *rescue workers* (judgement, +propriety) and *struggling to reach* (judgement,-capacity). The people on the rescue mission were appraised, resulting in the evoking of **judgement** in terms of **social sanction** and their behavior (i. e., 'struggling to reach') was appraised in terms of their capacity.

Appreciation concerns 'evaluations of semiotic and natural phenomena, according to the ways in which they are valued or not in a given field' (Martin & White, 2005, p. 43). For instance, the words *Typhoon Haiyan* occurring in both data sets revealed attitude toward the natural phenomenon in terms of its **composition** of wind. Similarly, some performances of the typhoon, such as *struck*, *hit*, and *slam* were also evaluated as **appreciation** of its 'impact', which engages people's attention. Table 23 shows the attitudinal choices identified in the two data sets.

Table 23 Comparison of Attitude Resource Distribution

Resource	CCTV News Update		BBC World News	
	f	%	*f*	%
Affect	24	12.84	5	5.05
Judgement	72	38.50	41	41.41
Appreciation	91	48.66	53	53.53
Totals	187	100.00	99	100.00

As shown in the table 23, both the CCTV and the BBC appeared to choose **appreciation** and **judgement** as their main attitudinal resources. **Appreciation** involved the evaluation of things, including natural phenomena, and their performance. This resource (48.66% of the CCTV choices and 53.53% of the BBC choices) was nearly equal to that of **judgement** (38.50% of the CCTV choices and 41.41% of the BBC choices). **Affect** was the least chosen resource in both data sets. These results indicated that news coverage of Typhoon Haiyan was devoted to the description of the participants (i.e., Typhoon Haiyan and its 'impact' and people and their behaviors in struggling with the typhoon).

However, the CCTV had a tendency to adopt more **affect** (12.84%) than did the BBC (5.05%), showing a more distinctive feature than the other case studies. More **affect** choices used by the CCTV could be attributed to the nature of the event. Unlike the human-agency events, such as the Syria Crisis, the Eurozone Crisis, or the Boston bombing, Typhoon Haiyan was resulted from nature, and this natural disaster seemed more important and consonant for Chinese people because it occurred in a neighboring country close to China and relevant to the Chinese people. In addition, the CCTV seemed to report the emotions of insecurity and unhappiness brought about by natural disasters. In addition, the CCTV expressed China's readiness to provide necessary assistance to the Philippines.

7.2.2 Attitudinal Polarity

To compare the operation of stance between the CCTV and the BBC, an examination of the polarity of attitudinal choices was necessary to understand the subtle dimensions with which these operate. Table 24 shows these dimensions and the distribution of the polarity of choices made by the two news organizations.

Table 24 Comparison of Polarity in the Subcategories of Attitudinal Resources

Resource subcategory	CCTV News Update				BBC World News			
	Negative		Positive		Negative		Positive	
	f	%	*f*	%	*f*	%	*f*	%
Affect								
●Security	1	0. 53	8	4. 28	0	0. 00	0	0. 00
●Satisfaction	0	0. 00	3	1. 60	0	0. 00	0	0. 00
●Inclination	5	2. 67	1	0. 53	1	0. 99	0	0. 00
●Happiness	1	0. 53	5	2. 67	0	0. 00	4	3. 96
●*Sub-total*	7	3. 73	17	9. 08	1	0. 99	4	3. 96
Judgement								
●Normality	1	0. 53	14	7. 49	0	0. 85	18	17. 82
●Capacity	4	2. 14	1	0. 53	5	4. 95	2	1. 98
●Tenacity	2	1. 07	2	1. 07	2	1. 98	2	1. 98
●Veracity	4	2. 14	1	0. 53	1	0. 99	0	0. 00
●Propriety	34	18. 18	9	4. 81	9	8. 91	2	1. 98
●*Sub-total*	45	24. 06	27	14. 43	17	17. 68	24	23. 76
Appreciation								
●Reaction	5	2. 67	53	28. 34	4	3. 96	38	37. 62
●Composition	4	2. 14	27	14. 44	0	0. 00	11	10. 89
●Valuation	0	0. 00	2	1. 07	1	0. 99	1	0. 99
●*Sub-total*	9	4. 81	82	43. 85	5	4. 95	50	49. 50
Totals	61	32. 60	126	67. 36	23	23. 62	78	77. 22

In general, the table shows both news programs held a

negative attitude towards the arrival of Typhoon Haiyan. However, choices in the resource of **judgement** varied somewhat between the CCTV and the BBC. In the CCTV data, the **judgement** was mostly involved with positive ethical behaviors (i. e., + propriety), with 45 of the 61 positive tokens identified as **Judgement**. The CCTV realized this attitude through wordings such as *rescue work ploughs on*, *international aid*, and *help with logistics and emergency communications systems*, which were evoked through contextual realization. In addition to the wide use of **judgement** in terms of propriety, the BBC also used the negative **judgement** of **normality** prominently. This might be related to reporting the people affected by the typhoon strike with inscribed words such as *those affected*, *death*, *fled their homes and cannot return* or neutral words such as *killed* and *missing*.

Another feature of **judgement** within the CCTV news coverage was the organization's preference for positive rather than negative evaluations. On the other hand, the BBC seemed to maintain a relatively balanced proportion between the binary polarities. Of note in the findings was the contrast in the use by the CCTV and the BBC of negative tokens in terms of propriety. The BBC seemed concerned with criticisms of the Philippine government's slow response to the typhoon and a range of activities, including Philippine officials blaming climate change, the dwindling of essential supplies, the misconduct of victims, and the Philippine's slow official response to the disaster. The focus of the negative **normality** in the BBC was mainly on the appraisal of the activities of those affected, which was taken as a breach of normal life.

The attitudinal choice of **appreciation** also seemed similar between the CCTV and the BBC, with both oriented to the negative aspect of things, especially in terms of **reaction** and **composition**. Thus, Typhoon Haiyan and its 'impact' or performance was negatively evaluated in the news discourse of both organizations.

In short, both broadcasters were very similar in appraising Typhoon Haiyan. The reporting reflected the negative tone of the typhoon as a devastating event, which was negatively appreciated. However, **judgement** in relation to people's actions in the face of the typhoon was positive.

7.2.3 Indirect Realization of Invoked Attitude: Evocations and Provocations

As elaborated in the previous chapters, **attitude** can be inscribed (i. e., explicitly articulated) or invoked (i. e., positioned less explicitly through evoking and provoking). White (2006) suggested that evocation, which refers to positive or negative assessment, is trigged by means of 'experiential [factual] material which has the potential to bring positive or negative reactions to the reader via attitudinal inference' (p. 40) ; provocation refers to positive or negative attitude provoked by formulations, ' which [although] evaluative, is not itself positive or negative, via intensification, comparison, metaphor or counter expectation' (White, 2006, p. 40).

Both the CCTV and the BBC realized attitude by the choice of some neutral lexis or formulations, as exemplified in the following extracts, as **invoked attitude** (either positive or negative, depending on the context) in their news coverage of Typhoon Haiyan.

Extract 7. 2. 1 (*CCTV News Update*)

> The country's disaster agency says 2,344 people are now known to have died[①] [judgement, -normality], nearly four thousand have been injured [judgement, -normality]. 79 people are officially listed as missing [judgement, -normality]. (14 – 11 – 2013)

Extract 7. 2. 2 (*BBC World News*)

> The official death toll [appreciation, -valuation] from the

① Note: The attitude invoked are designated by the elements underlined in order to be distinguished from the attitude inscribed indicated by bold letters.

typhoon Haiyan [appreciation,-reaction] has risen to over three and half thousand [appreciation,-reaction], although the UN says the figure could be much higher [appreciation,-reaction], the number of the people affected [judgement,-normality] has overall gone up to 11.8 million [appreciation,-reaction], at least 673,000 people [graduation, (force), quantification] have been displaced [judgement,-normality]. (15-11-2013)

Lexis such as *die*, *injure*, and *miss* were used in the CCTV data to describe victims suffering from Typhoon Haiyan. Lexis such as *higher* in the BBC data was used to evaluate 'the figure'. Both sets of choices were evoked by their contextual prosodies. Similarly, some formulations for the factual description of the situations in the typhoon-stricken areas (e.g., 'risen to over three and half thousand', 'gone up to 11.8 million' [used to evaluate *the death toll*], and the number of people affected (from *BBC World News* data set) were coded as evoked attitude. These experiential locutions could be used to trigger attitudinal positioning concerning the human cost of natural disasters by a process of inference.

The other indirect way of realizing **invoked attitude** is provocation. Some linguistic mechanisms or rhetorical devices were found in both data sets, including intensification, comparison, and metaphor. Intensification involves lexical choices that intensify the semantics (e. g. *super* as in 'super Typhoon Haiyan') in comparison with the other choices such as *big* or *strong*. Likewise the choices of *devastating* rather than *destroying*; the use of *rip through* instead of *destroy*, *break*, or *attack* (as in 'a devastating typhoon ripped through the central Philippines'), the use of *slam* versus *break* (as in 'super typhoon Haiyan slammed into the country on Friday') show the effect of intensification. In choosing lexis with intensifying semantics, news presenters accentuated the negative **appreciation** of Typhoon Haiyan.

Sometimes, the description of the typhoon-stricken areas was achieved via figurative speech or metaphor (shown in italics), as shown in the following extracts:

Extract 7. 2. 3 (*BBC World News*)

> There's no clear figure yet for the number of people who might have died, but the UN humanitarian chief has told the BBC world news many places look *as though they have experienced tsunami but huge boats are washed inland in the towns and villages*. (12 – 11 – 2013)

Extract 7. 2. 4 (*BBC World News*)

> A local congressman told the BBC the city of Tacloban is

like ground zero after a nuclear bomb explosion. (13 – 11 – 2013)

Other times the use of the discourse connective *but* in the textual composition not only facilitated transitional coherence in the discourse but also projected a counter claim and a contrasting expectation towards the prior proposition uttered. This also tended to provoke **attitude** for the viewers, as shown in Extract 7. 2. 5:

Extract 7. 2. 5 (*CCTV News Update*)

Government figures {for the death toll stand at 138 [appreciation, -reaction]. **But** the Philippine Red Cross says its field staff estimated the toll is about one thousand [appreciation, -reaction] in the hardest-hit [appreciation, -composition] Island of Leyate, with two hundred more casualties [affect, -happiness] in Samar province} . (11 – 11 – 2013)

In this case, the death toll reported between the Philippine government ('death toll stands at 138') and the Philippine Red Cross ('the toll is about one thousand') is contrasted through the use of *but*, which has a kind of evaluative positioning that intensifies the negative **appreciation** of the death toll. Thus, the factual report of the death toll might undergo an attitudinal assessment through a contrastive description.

Compared with the inscribed attitude, **invoked attitude** is the main mode, which realizes **attitude** in an implicit way. In the case of Typhoon Haiyan, the linguistic mechanism underlying the operation of stance was found to take the form of evocations that were realized via inference of the informational content and provocations, which were dependent on rhetorical devices such as intensification, comparison and contrast, and figurative speech. The reasons for being so might lie in the nature of the event. Typhoon Haiyan was not a human-agency disaster and reporting of this event relied on the description as rhetoric. In particular, the attitude of the news coverage was projected by focusing on the impact of the natural disaster.

7.3 Attribution as Realization of Stance in the News Coverage of Typhoon Haiyan

Attribution in the previous case studies was examined from several angles. For instance, journalistic alignment (authorial acknowledgement) and disalignment (authorial distancing) with attributed news propositions were examined via the choice of reporting words/verbs. Analysis of the evidential standing of the attributed propositions was achieved via recognition of source descriptors or the sayers. An investigation into the employment of attribution as a journalistic strategy in news practice was carried out to examine the degree to which news propositions were averred or attributed.

In this case study, the first step in this section of analysis was to identify the way in which attribution works linguistically in CCTV and BBC news coverage of Typhoon Haiyan. After that, the two organizations were compared in terms of their use of attribution as a way of realizing stance. The examination began with the identification of the reporting verbs used by the BBC and CCTV in each data set. These data are shown in Table 25 below.

Table 25 Comparison of Reporting Verbs

Verbs	CCTV News Update		BBC World News	
	f	%	*f*	%
Say (said/saying)	20	77.0	5	45.5
Report	3	11.5	0	0
Tell (told)	0	0.0	5	45.5
Add	1	3.8	0	0.0
Warn	2	7.7	0	0.0
Admit	0	0	1	9.0
Total	26	100.00	11	100.00

The table shows that CCTV adopted four reporting verbs: *say*, *report*, *add* and *warn*; the BBC adopted three: *say*, *report*, and *tell*. The verbs *say* and *report* were the main choices favored by the two broadcasters. These two verbs were evaluated as being more neutral in presenting authorial subjectivity to the attributed proposition.

However, reporting on the reporting verb *report* was somewhat problematic in that the word had two kinds of meaning in the transcribed texts, thus, the word worked on 'two planes of discourse' (Sinclair, 1981). One (type a) is the autonomous plane used to inform the audience of news information (i. e., what's happening); its source descriptor is one of the participants of the event (see Exs. 7. 3. 1 – 3). The other (type b) is the interactive plane, which deals with journalistic practice (e. g., telling the audience who sends the news report to the studio; see Ex. 7. 3. 4). The following extracts show the difference between the two:

Extract 7. 3. 1 (*CCTV News Update*)

> The U. S. Geological Survey is **reporting** that an earthquake with magnitude of 4. 8 has struck the municipality of San Isidro which is in the typhoon-affected Philippines. (12 – 11 – 2013)

Extract 7. 3. 2 (*CCTV News Update*)

Local residents **report** hearing gunshots near the San Juanico Bridge in Leyte on Wednesday. (14 – 11 – 2013)

Extract 7. 3. 3 (*CCTV News Update*)

Secretary General [of the Philippine Red Cross Gwendolyn Pang said the numbers came from preliminary **reports** by their teams at the two separate locations]. (10 – 11 – 2013)

Extract 7. 3. 4 (*CCTV News Update*)

But as CCTV correspondent Martin Lowe **reports** from there, is it stealing or survival? (15 – 11 – 2013)

In type a, *report* was used to introduce the news proposition toward the happening; In type b, the word was employed to indicate information about the field news reporter (e. g. , Martin Lowe), which gave little to the construction of news knowledge toward the happening.

The BBC's use of *report* was mainly on the interactive plane to show journalistic engagement with the audiences, to introduce follow-up news reports, and inform audiences that the news read in the studio was from the field news reporter, as shown in the following extracts:

Extract 7. 3. 5 (*BBC World News*)

Jon Donnison **reports** from there. (11 –11 –2013)

Extract 7. 3. 6 (*BBC World News*)

The BBC's Tim Willcox **reports** from the island of Cebu which has become a logistics hub for the UN aid operation. (12 –11 –2013)

In this sense, the use of *report* belonging to the second type was excluded from the analysis.

Reporting verbs of these types, although not actively presenting authorial support to the attributed proposition, were labeled as instances of authorial acknowledgement in this study rather than authorial distancing in appraisal theory, which shows an endorsement through the pattern of ' X says Y'. Therefore, analysis of the source descriptor (i. e. , figuring out the social status of the source) is always important in identifying the alignment made between the authorial voice and the attributed source

Additionally, the BBC used the word *tell* in introducing or reporting news propositions. This word has not been previously discussed in this dissertation. The following extracts show the BBC's use of tell:

Extract 7.3.7 (*BBC World News*)

There's no clear figure yet for the number of people who might have died, but the UN humanitarian chief has *told* **the BBC world news** many places look as though they have experienced tsunami but huge boats washed inland in the towns and villages. (12 – 11 – 2013)

Extract 7.3.8 (*BBC World News*)

A local congressman *told* **the BBC** the city of Tacloban is like ground zero after a nuclear bomb explosion. (13 – 11 – 2013)

Extract 7.3.9 (*BBC World News*)

Our correspondent Jonathan Head *told* **me** (news presenter) more about the aid situation in Tacloban, a city of more than two hundred thousand people, which was devastated by the storm. (14 – 11 – 2013)

Extract 7.3.10 (*BBC World News*)

To those affected, the secretary for the interior Mar Rojas has *told* **Rajesh Mirchandani** (BBC journalist), that Relief efforts had been delayed because of the scale of devastation. (15 – 11 – 2013)

Extract 7. 3. 11 (*BBC World News*)

Here's what the president *told* **my colleague Rajesh Mirchandani** (BBC journalist). (18 – 11 – 2013)

The use of *tell* seemed different from the uses of *say* and *report* because the authorial voice was not closely attached to the construction of the news in terms of evidential standing. *Tell* usually appeared within a pattern of reported speech (i. e., A tells B W). In this structure, A and B share the responsibility of ensuring the news proposition W is warrantable. The indirect object of *tell* in these extracts instances was identified as the journalistic voice (e. g., 'the BBC', 'me', 'Rajesh Mirchandani', etc.). Different from the neutral use of *say* and *report*, the journalistic voice was explicitly and actively engaged with the authorial construction of the news propositions. In other words, the journalist played a constructive role in the evidential standing of the news proposition.

Journalists can construct news via 'averral' declaring straightforwardly the facts about the reported event or 'attribution' to maintain the goal of journalistic objectivity. The neutral word *say* is the most direct and overt means for journalists to attribute news utterances to external sources.

However, its use in journalistic practice is by no means immune from stance taking or being absolutely objective. Thus, to discover how stance works implicitly through attribution, the use of neutral verb *say* was examined across the news texts. Table 26 shows the occurrence of *say* (*saying/said*) in all the clauses within the data sets.

Table 26 Comparison of Say Clauses

Program	No. of attributions through *say*		
	Total No. of clauses	*f*	%
CCTV	221	20	9.0
BBC	162	5	3.1

According to the table, the word *say* was the preferred strategy for CCTV in comparison with its use by the BBC. The CCTV used *say* in 9.0% of the clauses in the attribution of news knowledge about Typhoon Haiyan. The BBC used *say* in only 3.1% of its clauses. Therefore, attribution in the CCTV was manifested in the overuse of the neutral verb *say* to maintain objectivity strategically in comparison with the BBC.

However, stance can also be perceived through the investigation of source descriptors and the attributed propositions. Figuring out the source of news propositions was the first step in understanding the basis for news knowledge and its construction via journalistic alignment with the source. The *sayer* as source descriptor in the CCTV data set was found to have three identities in terms of geographical domains: domestic voices, such as the Philippine government; the voice of the aid organization, and voices from China and other international organizations. Table 27 shows the distribution of the *sayer* in the CCTV data set according to these three identities.

Table 27 Identification of the Sayer in the CCTV News Update Discourse

Identify of the sayer	Instances	*f*
Voice from the Philippines	He (Philippine President Benigno Aquino III); A regional police chief; Philippine; government officials; the Philippine Red Cross; Officials; The country's disaster agency; Authorities; The government; A spokesman for the Philippines' Foreign Ministry; Secretary General of the Philippine Red Cross Gwendolyn Pang;	11
Voice from China	Chinese Foreign Ministry spokesman Qin Gang; The foreign ministry; Foreign Ministry spokesman Hong Lei; Chinese Foreign Ministry Spokesman Hong Lei; He (Hong Lei); Hong Lei	6
Voice from international organizations	The United Nations World Food Programme; It (The United Nations World Food Programme); The World Meteorological Organization	3
Total		20

Information in Table 27 suggests that journalists considered the voices from the domestic government and official authorities in the Philippines to be the most warrantable and reliable source. The data also spotlighted the Chinese stance or attitude towards the typhoon's strike in the Philippines via diplomatic voices (e. g. , the Chinese Foreign Ministry or its spokesman). Six quotes from the Chinese diplomatic voice were mixed in with the news coverage of distant suffering, suggesting not only humanitarian value in the sending of international rescuers and supplies to the Philippines but also engagement with diplomatic or political color in reporting the natural disaster. The manifest embedding of the Chinese diplomatic voice in reporting the natural disaster served not only to profile China's international image but also to function as a defense against political doubts and criticisms from abroad concerning the lack of sufficient aid and assistance to the Philippines, as indicated in the following news item:

Extract 7. 3. 12 (*CCTV News Update*)

> The foreign ministry says China is set to provide another 10 million Yuan worth of relief supplies to the typhoon-hit Philippines. The supplies include tents and blankets, to be delivered soon. The announcement follows some questions

from abroad whether China is doing enough to help. (16 – 11 – 2013)

Hence, the intensive use of the Chinese voice in the CCTV discourse was somewhat different from the BBC news coverage. The *sayers* in the BBC news, although limited in quantity, were all from the Philippine government and the aid agencies.

In summary, attribution as realization of stance in the CCTV and the BBC news coverage suggested that authorial acknowledgement was established via the use of neutral reporting verbs such as *say* and *report*. However, it operated differently in the sense that the CCTV used the verb *say* more frequently to show its preference for external sources, which does not suggest active engagement with undertaking responsibility for news propositions. The use of the verb *tell* in the BBC data indicated shared responsibility between the journalists and the source. In other words, compared with *say*, *tell* indicated journalistic voice that was actively engaged with the attributed proposition.

The *sayers* of attributed propositions were identified as the domestic voice of the Philippines and outside voices such as the international voice of the United Nations and the diplomatic statements from China. The inclusion of the

Chinese voice by the CCTV indicated that the news discourse of reporting the natural disaster was imbued with political – diplomatic announcements and dialogue in the humanitarian communication.

7.4 Agency and Affectedness: The Case of Mediated Representation of Distant Suffering

Agency and affectedness as variables in the realization of stance in news reports of natural disasters can be explained by the following considerations: First, audiences are concerned with the representation of activities in such reports (i. e., what activities are reported and how they happened). Second, audiences want to know who are involved in these activities and why they are or are not identified to represent in those activities. To examine agency and affectedness in the case of Typhoon Haiyan, the material processes in SFG were selected as the tools for this analysis.

The results of analyzing attitudinal choices show (in section 2) that **judgement** and **appreciation** served as the main attitudinal choices in the operation of stance in this case study. This led to an assumption that the people and their behaviours were the focus of the linguistic evaluation. On the other hand, the action of the typhoon also underwent evaluation.

Thematically, the activities in both the CCTV and the BBC news reports were mainly concerned with the typhoon strike in the Philippines and the evacuation and rescue of the suffering. In this sense, the material processes in transitivity involving both kinds of activities (i. e., the material processes about the typhoon strike and about the rescue work) became interesting in terms of analysing the representation of this natural disaster across cultures. The material process in SFG (Halliday, 1994; Halliday & Matthiessen, 2004; Thompson, 1996) refers to a process of doing or happening in which the actor is the key participant and the material process of an action can be probed via the question 'what did the actor do?' or 'what happened?' To exemplify, the clauses concerning material processes were sorted out and placed in Appendix, some of which have been presented in Tables 28 and 29.

Table 28　Instances of Material Processes in CCTV News Update Coverage

Actor (agency)	Process (action)	Goal (affectedness)
1. Haiyan	To Enter	South China's Guangxi Zhuang Autonomous Region
2. Philippine President Benigno Aquino III	To Visit	A food aid distribution centre
3. It (The United Nations World Food Programme)	To Allocate	2 million US Dollars towards the relief work

(续上表)

Actor (agency)	Process (action)	Goal (affectedness)
1. China	To Send	Rescue and medical teams to the disaster-stricken areas in the Philippines
2. The devastation	To Kill	Nearly 4,000 people in the Philippines
3. They (A team of CCTV reporters)	To Meet	Rescuers from the Philippines and abroad
4. Climate change	To Cause	More such super storms

Table 29 Instances of Material Processes in BBC World News Coverage

Actor (agency)	Process (action)	Goal (affectedness)
1. A devastating typhoon	To rip through	The central Philippines
2. The united nations	Is appealing for	More than MYM300 million
3. The US	To send	An aircraft carrier and several other ships
4. Rescue workers	To reach	Many areas cut off by the storm
5. US air crafter carriers the George Washington	To arrive in	The Gulf of Leyte
6. The British navy	To deliver	Aid in the western Philippines
7. They (Christine Atillo-Villero and her family)	To survive	Typhoon Haiyan

The agency represented in the material process was responsible for action. In news coverage, the frequent selection of a certain type of material process may reveal a journalistic concern about the people involved in an action, preferably focused on what participants are involved in the event. Thus, the material processes concerning the activities of the typhoon strike and the rescue work were examined to identify how the agents in the active form of the processes were categorized, what type of agency was the preferred representation in the reporting of Typhoon Haiyan, and why this representation was selected.

The actors in the CCTV and the BBC data sets were classified into several categories: natural disaster; the activities performed by the Philippines, including the governments and its rescue units; the international organizations, such as the United Nations and its aid agencies; the activities relating to China; the activities relating to Britain; the activities relating to the United States; the activities done by the local residents; media; and other unspecified actors, such as climate change. For the purpose of comparison, the frequency of each category occurring in the CCTV and the BBC data sets has been shown in Table 30.

Table 30 Categorization of Agency

Categories of actors	*CCTV News Update*		*BBC World News*	
	f	%	*f*	%
Relating to the natural disaster of typhoon	9	23. 7	6	23. 1
The activities in relation to the Philippines	9	23. 7	8	30. 8
International organizations	3	7. 9	2	7. 7
The activities in relation to China	14	36. 8	0	0. 0
The activities in relation to Britain	0	0. 0	4	15. 4
The activities in relation to the US	0	0. 0	3	11. 5
The activities in relation to the resident	2	5. 3	2	7. 7
Media	1	2. 6	1	3. 8
Others (climate change)	2	5. 3	0	0. 0
Total	38	100. 0	26	100. 0

Both the CCTV and the BBC appeared to identify most of the actors in the material processes as agency relating to the natural disaster of the typhoon and to the voice of domestic assistance from the Philippines. The CCTV referred to the typhoon in 23. 7% of the instances found in the data. CCTV references to the domestic voice were also found in 23. 7% of the instances. The BBC referred to the natural disaster in 23. 1% of the instances and to the activities by the Philippines in 30. 8%. The actors categorized as the voice from the local residents were used less by both broadcasters.

Both broadcasters attached salient importance to the factual information about the typhoon, which brought devastating impacts to the region attacked. The organizations also projected the responsive rescue work undertaken by the Philippines government. In terms of journalist practice, the CCTV and the BBC seemed similar in their projecting of the natural disaster to their news audiences, which was to evaluate the natural disaster and its impacts on the people and the governmental endeavors to respond to the natural attack. Thus, the people in the stricken area were depicted as the affected, who were offered aid and various forms of assistance. The tension formed between the natural disaster, represented as the actor that caused varying devastating effects to ordinary residents, and the governmental activities represented as the dispatcher to ordinary residents. Thus, both the CCTV and the BBC shaped the government as the authoritative voice with a leading role in rescuing the people from the natural crisis. In contrast, the people as ordinary residents in the action were less represented in fighting against the natural disaster in the coverage of both organizations.

Other differences in the coverage were also found. For instance, the activity in relation to China in the reporting of a distant suffering was one of the salient observations in the CCTV news coverage. This process of mediation of distant suffering (Chouliaraki, 2008) involved political claims and interest, as shown in the following extract:

Extract 7.4.1 (*CCTV News Update*)

> **China** is considering the Philippine's current situation and needs, **China** will dispatch medical assistance to the disaster-hit areas. Some medical rescue groups registered under the Chinese Red Cross have expressed their willingness to help. **China** has been paying close attention to the disaster in the Philippines. **China** has repeatedly stated its decision to provide humanitarian aid to the Philippines. **China** is keeping in close contact with the Philippine government to make sure supplies can be delivered safely. (17 - 11 - 2013)

This extract shows that a transnational flow of information flow existed within the news discourse. China as the agency of a series of material processes repeatedly positioned itself as a humanitarian actor in humanitarian communication. Seen from the processes of action, China was profiled in the news discourse as a dispatcher for disaster relief. This profile was constructed from the perspective of a spectator of the distant suffering. Rather than using emotion-oriented discourse to mobilize blame for those factoring in the suffering, the CCTV exposed China's political claim to offer aid initiatives to the under-represented people as beneficiary. Thus, the agency assumed by the voice from China was featured in the CCTV news coverage. This was not found in the BBC news coverage. Thus, commitments of media institutions, no matter what their audiences, may vary in terms of their social contexts. In this case, although oriented to the international audience, the English program on the CCTV *News Update* appeared to speak for Chinese national interests. This was in contrast with the BBC *World News*, which spotlighted internal community conflict in its reporting of the distant suffering.

Another similarity found in the coverage of both organizations was the distinguishing of two kinds of participants: animate and inanimate. Apart from some animate agents, including the Philippine government, the people affected, China, and medical rescue groups, both organizations included inanimate agents in their coverage (e. g., Typhoon Haiyan, the rescue work, the devastation).

Typhoon Haiyan was represented as a natural disaster in both the CCTV and the BBC news reports, a mediation of distant suffering that involved an external threat to a community. Although the disaster as agent was an outside factor from the human community, the disaster victims usually personalized this agent as if they were talking about an animate attacker through the use of ' rip through', for example, ' Typhoon Haiyan ripped through the Philippines'. This personalization was associated not only with news reporting rhetoric but also with authorial stance, which was hidden behind the text.

The representation of the typhoon as an animate participant in both the CCTV and the BBC news reports as an agent of an action was particularly characteristic of reporting natural disasters. In giving inanimate participants agency, news presenters could profile the devastating power of the typhoon and frame opposing tension between the natural disaster and the affected. If agency is the assumed ' doer' of an action and affectedness is the recipient of that action, then an inanimate attacker such as a typhoon is personalized as the doer as shown in these phrases taken from the data sets: ' Typhoon Haiyan struck central islands in the Philippines' and ' a devastating typhoon ripped through the centre of the Philippines'. However, this personalized representation of natural disasters in journalistic practice has also been the subject of questions concerning whether an existing conflict is muted by talking about the disaster agents as if they are human beings (Dynes & Quarantelli, 1976).

7.5 Conclusions and Discussion

Attitude, attribution, and agency versus affectedness as the variables were investigated to explore the linguistic realization of stance in both the CCTV and the BBC television news coverage. The findings suggested that attitudinal stance to the Typhoon Haiyan was represented as negative by both broadcasters. Similar attitudinal choices concerning **judgement** and **appreciation** were adopted by both news programs. This indicated that the CCTV and the BBC news coverage were concerned with the appraisal of people and their acts and the evaluation of things (i. e., the phenomenal happening of a natural disaster and its devastation). One of the contrastive features between the CCTV and the BBC was CCTV's dedication to a positive **judgement** of the people and the people's actions in the dimension of propriety. This meant that the CCTV instilled a positive stance into its coverage of the rescue work from various sources, even though maintaining a negative color in the overall news report. The BBC seemed to focus on both positive **propriety** and negative **normality** concerning the breach of the affected's normative life. **Attitude** as realization of stance was detected in both evocations and provocations, two subtypes of **invoked attitude**. This suggested that the operation of stance not only lay in the semantics of evaluative lexis inscribed in text but also relies on implicit attitudinal inference and rhetorical effects that these formulations created. The findings revealed that the invoked attitude operated by way of the semantic identification of lexical choice, the use of figurative speech, and the use of counter-claims.

Attribution was one of the mechanisms used to realize stance in this case and was explored in respect of the organizations' choices of reporting words. The CCTV and the BBC both used neutral reporting words frequently, especially the verbs *say* and *report*. However, *report* worked on two different planes of discourse, one of which contributed to the construction of the news propositions regarding the event and the other of which worked on the plane of interactive discourse. A comparison of the verb *tell*, used exclusively in the BBC coverage, and the verb *say*, preferred in the CCTV coverage, suggested the pattern of *tell* was more prone to journalistic intervention in relation to the news propositions as well as the construction of news knowledge. However, use of the reporting verb *say* by no means assumed news presenters were refraining from journalistic subjectivity. Thus, the *sayers* in the pattern of attribution of *say*, as manifested in the CCTV, were investigated.

The categories of *sayer* were identified as the internal voice from the Philippines community and the external voices from international aid organizations and China. CCTV's inclusion of China's voice in the reporting of Typhoon Haiyan, was imbued with a transitional information flow with an emphasis on political-diplomatic statements in the news communication.

Finally, the variable of agency versus affectedness was explored in both the CCTV and the BBC coverage using the material process in the transitivity network of SFG. The material processes encoding both the represented activities of the typhoon strike and the rescue work were sorted to determine what agencies were represented as liable for the acts and the relevant reasons for that representation. Initially, the actors in the material processes were categorized into several types (i. e., the natural disaster of typhoon, internal voice from the Philippines, and so on). Then, as participants in the material processes, most of actors were identified as agency relating to the natural disaster of the typhoon and to the agency in relation to domestic assistance from the Philippines. This was a salient feature manifested in both the CCTV and the BBC news coverage. However, the CCTV differed from the

BBC in that the CCTV also attributed most of the agencies to concepts relating to the external source, China. In doing so, the CCTV shed journalistic detachment over the activities carried out by China and the Chinese government.

Chapter 8 Discussion and Conclusions

This chapter draws together a series of threads that run throughout the study. It then draws some conclusions as well as noting the limitations of the study and its contributions to the body of research.

8.1 Further Discussion

Several threads have emerged over the course of the four case studies presented out in the previous chapters. The foci in the following discussion are attitudinal stance and attribution in the CCTV and the BBC news coverage.

8.1.1 Overviewof the Attitudinal Stance across the Case Studies

This section is an examination of the different attitudinal categories adopted in each event reported by CCTV and the BBC to compare their operation of attitudinal stance. Table 31 contains a summary of the attitude systems operating throughout the four cases in the CCTV news discourse.

Table 31 Attitude Variations in the CCTV News Discourse of the Four Cases

Subset of the CCTV corpora	Affect		Judgement		Appreciation		Totals	
	f	%	*f*	%	*f*	%	*f*	%
Syria crisis	50	16. 23	186	60. 39	72	23. 38	308	100. 00
Eurozone crisis	35	22. 15	59	37. 34	64	40. 51	158	100. 00
Boston bombing	15	14. 85	54	53. 47	32	31. 68	101	100. 00
Typhoon Haiyan	24	12. 84	72	38. 50	91	48. 66	187	100. 00

The table shows variations in the three **attitude** choices in the CCTV news coverage from one case to another. One common feature is that the option of **affect** remained the least favored choice. The other two options of **judgement** and **appreciation** also play an important role in construction of attitudinal stance. These, however, vary in their application according to the nature of events, which of course not equivalent across the course of the news coverage. Conversely, **judgement** seems to be preferably used (with a ratio of 60. 39 % and 53. 47% in its proportional distribution respectively) in the cases of the Syria Crisis and the Boston Bombing. These two events are human-agency activities in their nature and thus typically associated with appraising people's behaviors. In addition, **appreciation** and **judgement** were relatively close in their proportional distribution in the cases of the Eurozone Crisis and the Typhoon Haiyan. This could be because those two events were not human-made activities. For instance, the Eurozone crisis took place in the economic domain of social life, which could not be directly caused by people. Similarly, Typhoon Haiyan was a natural disaster, far from the control of people.

The examination reveals that stance variations occur throughout the news coverage of the four different events in the CCTV news discourse. The dimension of **attitude** may be allocated in terms of the nature of the events and the habitus of journalistic practice. First, in the cases of the Syria Crisis and the Boston Bombing, CCTV attaches the focus to the victims; the people ready to rescue and to give assistance are also subject to evaluation. Therefore, suffering and the offering of aid are the twin themes for reporting human-made calamities. This reporting of human-made calamities projects journalistic sympathy to the innocent victims in contrast to the condemnation of people who commit wrong doing against human beings. second, a different treatment in the natural calamity, the Typhoon Haiyan, appears to exist in the tying together of **judgement** and **appreciation**. This indicates that the phenomena due to the natural devastation are evaluated along with the people who are suffering or who are ready to help. Evaluations targeting both the state of world and its people in the news of the natural calamity refract a compassionate **attitude** towards the affected in the pitiful conditions.

Table 32 summarizes the proportional distribution of choices in the BBC news discourse across the four cases.

Table 32 Attitude Variations in the BBC News Discourse of the Four Cases

Subset of the BBC corpora	Affect		Judgement		Appreciation		Totals	
	f	%	*f*	%	*f*	%	*f*	%
Syria crisis	61	20. 13	148	48. 85	94	31. 03	303	100. 00
Eurozone crisis	36	36. 00	34	34. 00	30	30. 00	100	100. 0
Boston bombing	25	18. 66	65	48. 51	44	32. 84	134	100. 00
Typhoon Haiyan	5	5. 05	41	41. 41	53	53. 53	99	100. 00

The table suggests that among the three **attitude** systems, **judgement** is the prominent resource employed in BBC news coverage, although a slight divergence exists between **judgement** and **appreciation** in some cases . The percentage of **judgement** identified in the cases of the Syria Crisis, the Boston Bombing, represent almost half of the BBC's attitudinal choices. The shared traits of these cases are their destructive in nature and the threat to people's normal lives. The favorable use of **judgement** suggests that BBC is more focused on the people and their behaviours involved in these crises.

Compared with the other two **attitude** systems, **affect** is not favored in any of the four cases. The BBC seems to avoid **affect** in the coverage of the Typhoon Haiyan, in contrast with its coverage of the Eurozone Crisis, the percentages of **affect** reported in these cases is 36% (the Eurozone crisis) and 5.05% (the Typhoon Haiyan), respectively, a substantial difference. This contrast may be because of the news value of proximity of the events. In other words, the Eurozone crisis was more geographically close to Britain than Typhoon Haiyan, thus, more consonant to British people's concern. **Affect** was a relatively favored choice for the BBC to report the consequences of the Eurozone Crisis to engage the audience. British people care more about consequential changes that austerity measures may bring to their normal lives than other respects of the story, such as the official summits and their discussions (unlike the treatment in the CCTV program). Therefore, the emotional responses of the ordinary people afflicted by the Eurozone Crisis, such as the affective mental and behavioral processes, are highly regarded by the BBC journalists in arousing consonance. The Typhoon Haiyan, which occurred in the Philippines, was geographically distant from the BBC. Thus, its environmental impacts (the devastation of the calamity) may have been seen as the aspects relevant to the audience's lives.

To conclude, stance variations of the events both in CCTV and BBC coverage can be linked in two respects. First, the choice of the **attitude** is dependent upon the universally perceived moral values towards the events or the happenings. Namely, people from different parts of world normally tend to appraise acts of offering help to those affected by disasters positively; similarly, people may hold a negative **attitude** towards acts threatening people's lives. Second, the choice of **attitude** may be related to the sociocultural differences in which the journalistic practice is exercised.

Table 33 summarizes the **attitude** polarity revealed in the CCTV and BBC data sets for the four cases.

Table 33 Polarity of Attitude in the CCTV and the BBC News Discourse of the Four Cases

Sub-set of the BBC corpora	CCTV News Update				BBC World News			
	Positive		Negative		Positive		Negative	
	f	%	*f*	%	*f*	%	*f*	%
Syria Crisis	108	35. 07	200	**64. 93**	105	34. 65	198	**65. 34**
Eurozone Crisis	85	**53. 79**	73	**46. 26**	47	**47. 00**	53	**53. 00**
Boston Bombing	30	36. 96	71	**63. 04**	33	26. 60	91	**73. 40**
Typhoon Haiyan	61	32. 60	126	**67. 40**	23	23. 62	78	**77. 22**

Note: The percentage shown in bold indicates the basic key (where it is positive or negative) toned for each case in the CCTV and the BBC news.

This table shows that the CCTV and the BBC shared similar polarities of attitude in the four events. The basic key to whether the **attitude** is positive or negative in each case is indicated through one polar value outweighing another. Therefore, the percentage shown in bold indicates the basic key (where it is positive or negative) toned for each case in the CCTV and the BBC news. Both the CCTV and the BBC as institutional voices hold negative attitudes towards the Syria Crisis, the Boston Bombing, and the Typhoon Haiyan. In the case of the Eurozone Crisis, the attitude is fine tuned to be either positive or negative across CCTV and BBC coverage.

To summarize, the attitudinal stances realized in the CCTV and the BBC reporting across the four cases are not strikingly divergent or conflicting in terms of negative or positive attitude toward the events, but in very different ways, working in the categories of attitude.

8.1.2 Overview of Attribution in the CCTV and the BBC News Presentation Discourse

In this section, **attribution** is discussed as the realization of stance operation in the discourse of television news presentations of the four cases. News utterances that are averred by journalists or attributed to other sources position their audiences differently. Averral is often assumed to make the voice in the text more monologic, whereas attribution opens up a possibility of being polyphonic. In **Appraisal** Theory, **attribute** is distinguished as two types, distancing and acknowledging, in terms of the use of reporting words (e. g., the use of *claim* vs. *believe*). Going beyond this distinction, attribution as a linguistic device in the realization of stance can be explored through appraising the source descriptors and the attributed statements. In addition, the greater or lesser use of attribution in the texts suggests whether the text is actively positioned dialogically or not. The intent of this discussion is to determine to what extent news informational knowledge (across broadcasters) is constructed via attributed clauses. To do this requires an understanding of the definition of a clause in terms of news texts.

The definitional concepts of a clause vary in English grammar and linguistics (Biber et al., 1999; Crystal, 1997; Kroeger, 2005; Radford, 2004). The notion of clause in *Longman Grammar of Spoken and Written English* (Biber et al., 1999) is applied to the work on the present data. Biber and his fellow scholars attempted to approach clause from a discoursal perspective by distinguishing the different types of clauses in language use, basically either main clauses or embedded clauses.

Extract 8. 1. 1 shows how an item of news information is segmented into a cluster of clauses:

Extract 8. 1. 1 (*BBC World News*)

(1) The Jordanian government has nearly doubled its estimates of the amount of money (2) it needs (3) to cope with the influx of refugees from Syria. (4) In an appeal issued jointly with the United Nations, (5) *Jordan says* (6) *it urgently needs seven-hundred million dollars*. (7) More than a hundred and eighty thousand Syrians are currently sheltering in Jordan. (8) The country is struggling (9) to meet their needs. [Gale Gavlick reports from Amman]. (02 –09 –2012)

The whole extract contains nine clauses, each numbered for reference. Clauses 2, 3, 6, and 9 are embedded in main clauses 1, 5, 7 and 8. The italicized clauses signal attributions to external sources as indicated by the word *say* indicating the information was reported by Jordan. Thus, clauses 5 and 6 are grouped as attributable clauses. The results of the examination of attribution in the whole CCTV and BBC texts are shown in Table 34.

Table 34 Distribution of Attribution in the CCTV and BBC News Discourses

	CCTV News Update		*BBC World News*	
Subset of the corpora	No. of news propositional clauses	No. of attributed propositional clauses (%)	No. of news propositional clauses	No. of attributed propositional clauses (%)
1. Syria crisis	655	300 (45.80)	418	121 (28.95)
2. Eurozone crisis	161	66 (40.99)	153	19 (12.42)
3. Boston bombing	151	58 (38.41)	205	55 (26.83)
4. Typhoon Haiyan	221	92 (41.63)	162	32 (19.75)
Totals	1,254	535 (42.66)	1,066	247 (23.17)

On average, the total count of clauses attributable in the CCTV news coverage was 535 of a total of 1,254 with a percentage of 42.66%. This is considerably higher than the 23.17% in the BBC, where there was 247 clauses of a total of 1,066. These figures indicate that CCTV uses more attributions than the BBC, suggesting CCTV news is prone to attributing news information to other sources. In contrast, the BBC news tends to aver news information rather than to attribute it to the other sources.

Indeed, an issue of "objectivity" and "impartiality" is at stake. Although attribution is usually recognized as a strategic ritual adopted by journalists to achieve a sense of objectivity (Tuchman, 1972), this ritual is not simply equivalent to being objective. In fact, attribution as a journalistic strategy is treated as ‘doing objectivity’. Therefore, it is problematic to claim the journalists from the CCTV are more objective than those from the BBC in their news practice.

Moreover, the table suggests that, on average, 42.66% of the CCTV news knowledge is constructed on the basis of the reported speech of other sources, with the authorial stance of the whole institutional discourse buried within many different quotes. This raises the problem as to whether the frequent use of attribution may potentially undermine the authorial voice of a broadcaster. When the institutional voice assumed to be authoritative for the audience is hybridized with other external voices, its accomplished authority becomes problematic.

8.2 Conclusions

First, the findings from this study reveal the attitudinal stances realized in the CCTV and the BBC across the four cases vary in a different ways in terms of the categories of attitude, although the attitudinal stances are not strikingly divergent or conflicting in terms of negative or positive attitude toward these events. For instance, analysis of the four cases showed attitudinal stance is realized differently from one event to another. For example, attitudes toward the events varied in terms of the proportional distributions of attitudinal categories (i. e. , **affect**, **judgment**, **appreciation**) and in their subcategories or dimensions of diverse kinds. In addition, the comparative survey revealed linguistic mechanisms of attitudinal stance worked differently between the CCTV and the BBC.

Second, the focus of this present study was not only to show in what subtle ways the variations of attitude toward the different events are realized for the two broadcasters but also to identify the variables that **affect** the attitudinal homogenization within the international communication of news information between the CCTV and the BBC. Two reasons account for this observation. One reason is that the polarities of attitude to the events are determined by the nature of the events. The other may be because the CCTV and the BBC news practice in the same news culture: the international news culture.

This finding seems to depart from the pre-established expectation that the CCTV and the BBC, respectively regarded as Eastern and Western media and two culturally distinct institutions, will diverge greatly in attitudinal stance operating cross cultures. In other words, arriving at a generalization concerning striking differences in attitudinal stance operation between the CCTV and the BBC is simple matter, although some deviations were detected. In principle, the CCTV and the

BBC tend to converge in shared value positions to given events; thus, their news representations contain no strikingly contradictory attitudes. The possible causes for this are multifaceted, one of which may be related to the limitation of data selection. Apart from the differing constructs of news values for this case, the other selected events took place outside the broadcasters' affiliated countries (i. e., China and Britain). Thus, both organizations reported these events from the perspective of distant spectators. The perspective of distant spectators was more external than directly aligned or disaligned with any party in the events. Another possible reason may be associated with news practice. A usual practice for CCTV English news is its use of external news agencies as sources in the reporting of international events. Re-editing, reformulating, and even directly referring to the news media from which the news is sourced (e. g., Reuters, Associated Press, etc.) has become the primary source for the CCTV English news channel. The following two extracts show this use of external sources:

Extract 8. 2. 2 (*CCTV News Update*, Syria Crisis)

> Welcome back to CCTV news, now let's check out all the matters surrounding Syria: The Syrian Army is calling on residents of the restive Homs suburb of Jeb al-Jandali to return

home, after claiming to have cleared the neighborhood of anti-regime fighters. **AP** { **footage** of the suburb shows deserted streets and gutted buildings. } (14 – 10 – 2012)

Extract 8. 2. 3 (*CCTV News Update*, Eurozone Crisis)

Spanish Prime Minister Mariano Rajoy has said a request for European aid is not imminent. **It comes after a Reuters** {report, citing European Union sources, said the country could request help as early as next weekend}. (02 – 10 – 2012)

Therefore, sourcing from foreign mainstream English-media such as the Associated Press and Reuters and re-editing these sources have become constant news practices for CCTV English news (Liang & Xie, 2010). This may give rise to a homogenization of the stance working in the CCTV news contents with that of the Western news media, such as the BBC. This news practice may also be the explanation for CCTV news being prone to construct attribution.

Third, the most revealing difference in stance taking between the CCTV and the BBC lies in the intersubjective positioning realized in their news discourse practices. CCTV seemed to make news communication more polyphonic by attributing news propositions to external sources; the BBC tended to aver news propositions. This conclusion was based on the comparison of the percentage of attributable propositional clauses among all the clauses for each of the news organizations. In this sense, the CCTV seems more detached from its news propositions by attempting to be more 'objective' through using quotes and citations from other sources. Conversely, the BBC is more attached to an authorial voice in news delivery and tends to aver news information as an authoritative source. Nonetheless, news organizations can realize stance through the social roles of attributed sources (i.e., source descriptors; White, 2012), the meanings coded in attributed propositions, and even in the discourse practice of attribution.

Fourth, to be more comprehensive, this study not only was based on **Appraisal** theory and but also drew upon other linguistic resources, attempting to be comprehensive through exploring the discursive representation of the participants in the selected case studies as agency and affected involved with typical activity.

8.3 Contributions and Limitations

By virtue of using Appraisal to analyze stance, we are able to show in detailed ways the variations between different broadcasters in the way they perform the journalistic task of 'doing' objectivity. The practice of journalism in television news presentations was assumed to be an ideal site to exercise the norms of objectivity through the delivery of news presentation to audiences because of the restrictions imposed in the synoptic writing of news information concerning news professionals' attachment of personal voices. On one hand, the belief that all language use is not value-free should be of interest for linguists and discourse analysts in exploring stance realization in narrowly confined news texts to uncover authorial intervention in those texts. On the other hand, methodologically, **appraisal** theory, an effective analytic tool in the study of stance, has been applied to texts in diverse genres but rarely to the discourse of television news presentation. The aim of this research was to marry television news presentation discourse and appraisal theory to bear out the methodological applicability.

The comparison between the CCTV and the BBC television news discourse was the first attempt at discourse analysis to form a mosaic of the significant linguistic devices used to express evaluation and stance. Conducting such studies should be worthwhile because through a comparative perspective not only similarities and differences across languages and cultures (CCTV and BBC are two culturally distinct media institutions) can be revealed but also the ways in which television news is constructed and event reporting is carried out in highly profiled broadcast platforms can be determined. In this study, the choices of the BBC and the CCTV for comparison were appropriate because the BBC is a highly regarded and internationally known news institution and CCTV is an emerging and increasingly influential news organization in the age of globalization.

Last but not least, the study revealed the efficacy of combining White's framework as extended from **appraisal** theory and SFL to the 'reporter voice' style of news. Using these qualitative tools of discourse analysis resulted in providing greater insight into a complex linguistic phenomenon.

Nevertheless, this research was not without some limitations.

First, in methodological terms, appraisal theory was applied as the analytic tool to examine the realizations of stance in the television news presentations. The distinction between inscribed and invoked attitudes is informed by appraisal theory. Appraisal theory well demonstrated the identification and coding issues of the inscribed attitude; however, some constraints apply when working with the implicit realization of attitude in the data coding for this present study. In particular were determining the length of linguistic units in which implicit attitudes were identified and coded. For example, *kill* in the case of '15 people have been killed when a **booby-trapped** car exploded' is an invoked attitude working with other linguistic elements—such as 15 *people* [*dead*] and a booby-trapped car—in its context, but determining attitude by coding as a unit the lexis *kill* or the longer clause 15 *people have been killed* was a challenge. The issue of how coders can avoid such difficulty has not been systematically addressed in appraisal theory. Thus, the reliability of coding and avoidance of the researcher's subjectivity deserve consideration for future research.

Second, the theme of this research was to determine variations in stance between the CCTV and the BBC news presentations. However, the CCTV news data were selected from the English language news rather than from the Chinese language news. Expanding the study to compare the operation of stance in television news presentation across languages would be more insightful, although more challenging. Doing so might also involve revisions to methodology.

Finally, some of the corpora built for comparison were relatively limited in size for conducting a diachronic study. In other words, more data would be needed to adopt a longitudinal perspective for such case studies as the case of the Syria Crisis, which has continuous warfare, to show how stance diachronically changes in the news coverage. In addition, the data selection needed to be more comprehensive and more representative to prevent the comparative study from being confined to qualitative exploration and to open it to quantitative methodologies, such as corpus linguistics. More comprehensive data could also have resulted in the use of more technologically assisted computational devices. In addition to these suggestions, a comparison of the BBC and the CCTV reports against a reference text would have helped to enrich the present study. Thus, using a reference text from another English-speaking news organization, such as CNN, to compare variations of stance realized across the BBC and CCTV would possibly strengthen future studies.

References

Alba-Juez, L. & Thompson, G. (2014). The many faces and phases of evaluation. In G. Thompson & L. Alba-Juez (Eds.), *Evaluation in Context* (pp. 3 – 24). Amsterdam: John Benjamins.

Allan, S. (1998). News from nowhere: Televisual news discourse and the construction of hegemony. In A. Bell and P. Garrett (Eds.), *Approaches to Media Discourse* (pp. 105 – 141). Oxford: Blackwell Publishers.

Anthonissen, C. (2003). Interaction between visual and verbal communication: Changing patterns in the printed media. In G. Weiss and R. Wodak (Eds.), *Critical Discourse Analysis: Theory and interdisciplinarity* (pp. 297 – 311). Basingstoke: Palgrave Macmillan.

Becker, A. (2009). Modality and engagement in British and German TV interviews. In K. Aijmer (Ed.), *Contrastive Pragmatics* (pp. 5 – 22). Amsterdam: John Benjamins.

Bednarek, M. (2006a). *Evaluation in Media Discourse: Analysis of a newspaper corpus*. London: Continuum.

Bednarek, M. (2006b). Epistemological positioning and evidentiality in English news discourse: A text-driven approach. *Text & Talk*, 26 (6), 635 – 660.

Bednarek, M. (2008). *Emotion Talk across Corpora*. New York: Palgrave Macmillan.

Bednarek, M. (2009). Language patterns and attitude. *Functions of Language*, 16 (2), 165 – 192.

Bednarek, M. (2011). Expressivity and televisual characterization. *Language and Literature*, 20 (1), 3 – 21.

Bednarek, M. & Caple, H. (2012). *News Discourse*, London: Continuum.

Bednarek, M. & Caple, H. (2014). Why do news values matter? Towards a new methodological framework for analysing news discourse in critical discourse analysis and beyond. *Discourse & Society*, 25 (2), 135 – 158.

Bell, A. (1991). *The Language of News Media*. Oxford:

Blackwell publishers.

Biber, D. & Finegan, E. (1988). Adverbial stance types in English. *Discourse Processes*, 11 (1), 1 – 34.

Biber, D. & Finegan, E. (1989). Styles of stance in English: Lexical and grammatical marking of evidentiality and affect. *Text and Talk*, 9 (1)93 – 124.

Biber, D., Johansson, S., Leech, G., Conrad, S. & Finegan, E. (1999). *Longman Grammar of Spoken and Written English*. London: Longman.

Billig, M. (2008). The language of critical discourse analysis. *Discourse and Society*, 19 (6), 783 – 800.

Boczkowski, P. J. (2009). Rethinking hard and soft news production: From common ground to divergent paths. *Journal of Communication*, 59 (1), 98 – 116.

Boltanski, L. (1999). *Distant Suffering: Politics, morality and the media*. Cambridge: Cambridge University Press.

Bombelli, G. Soler, L. R. & Waasaf, M. S. (2013). The

language of evaluation: Paralinguistic features as a phonological domain for appraisal. *DELTA: Documentasão de Estudos em Lingüística Teórica e Aplicada*, 29 (2), 267 – 280.

Busà, M. G. (2013). *Introducing the Language of the News: A student's guide*. London: Routledge.

Caldas-Coulthard, C. R. (2003). Cross-cultural representation of 'otherness' in media discourse. In G. Weiss and R. Wodak (Eds.), *Critical Discourse Analysis: Theory and interdisciplinary* (pp. 272 – 296). Basingstoke: Palgrave Macmillan.

Calsamiglia, H. & Ferrero, C. L. (2003). Role and position of scientific voices: Reported speech in the media. *Discourse Studies*, 5 (2), 147 – 173.

Caffarel, A. & Rechniewski, E. (2008). When is a handover not a handover? A case study of ideologically opposed French news stories. In E. Thomson & P. R. R. White (Eds.), *Communicating Conflict: Multilingual case studies of the news media* (pp. 25 – 50). London: Continuum.

Chiluwa, I. & Ifukor, P. (2015). War against our children: Stance and evaluation in # BringBackOurGirls campaign discourse on Twitter and Facebook. *Discourse & Society*, 26 (3), 267 – 296.

Chouliaraki, L. (2008). The mediation of suffering and the vision of a cosmopolitan public. *Television & New Media*, 9 (5), 371 – 391.

Chouliaraki, L. (2006). *The Spectatorship of Suffering*. London: Sage.

Clayman, S. E. (1988). Displaying neutrality in television news interviews. *Social Problems*, 35 (4), 474 – 492.

Clayman, S. (1992). Footing in the achievement of neutrality: The case of news interview discourse. In P. Drew and J. Heritage (Eds.), *Talk at Work* (pp. 163 – 198). Cambridge: CUP.

Clayman, S. (2002). Disagreements and third parties: Dilemmas of neutralism in panel news interview. *Journal of Pragmatics* 34 (10 – 11), 1385 – 1401.

Clayman, S. & Heritage, J. (2002). *The News Interview: Journalists and public figures on the air*. Cambridge: CUP.

Cohen, E. (1992). *Philosophical Issues in Journalism*. New York: Oxford University Press.

Collins Collins Cobuild (2007). *Collins Cobuild Advanced American English Dictionary*. Boston: Cengage Learning.

Conrad, S. & Biber, D. (2000). Adverbial marking of stance in speech and writing. In S. Hunston & G. Thompson (Eds.), *Evaluation in Text: Authorial stance and the construction of discourse* (pp. 56 – 73). Oxford: OUP.

Corner, J. (1999). *Critical Ideas in Television Studies*. New York: Oxford University Press.

Clift, R. (2006). Indexing stance: Reported speech as an interactional evidential. *Journal of Sociolinguistics*, 10 (5), 569 – 595.

Crystal, D. (1997). *A Dictionary of Linguistics and Phonetics* (4th ed.). Oxford: Blackwell Publishers.

Dennis, E. E. (1984). Journalistic objectivity is possible. In E. E. Dennis & J. C. Merrill (Eds.), *Basic Issues in Mass Communication: A debate* (pp. 111 – 118). New York:

Macmillan.

Downing, L. H. (2006). The expression of writer stance by modal adjectives and adverbs in comparable corpus of English and Spanish newspaper discourse. In A. M. Hornero, M., Luzón, J., & Ornat, S. M. (Eds.), *Corpus Linguistics: Applications for the study of English* (pp. 125 – 140). New York: Peter Lang.

Du Bois, J. (2004). Searching for intersubjectivity: 'too' and 'either' in stance alignment. In *25th Conference of the International Computer Archive of Modern and Medieval English*, Verona: University of Verona.

Du Bois, J. (2007). The stance triangle. In R. Englebretson (Ed.), *Stance-taking in Discourse* (pp. 139 – 182). Amsterdam: John Benjamins.

Dynes, R. & Quarantelli E. (1976). Community conflict: its absence and its presence in natural disasters. *Mass Emergencies*, (1), 139 – 152.

Eggins, S. & Slade, D. (1997). *Analysing Casual Conversation*. London: Equinox Publishing Ltd.

Ekström, M. & Kroon Lundell, A. (2011). Beyond the broadcast interview: Specialized forms of interviewing in the making of television news. *Journalism Studies*, 12 (2), 172 – 187.

Elorza, I. (2009). Positioning readers in newspaper discourse: A contrastive case study. *Birkbeck Studies in Applied Linguistics*, 4: 1 – 22.

Entman, R. M. (1991). Framing U. S. coverage of international news: Contrasts in narratives of the KAL and Iran air incidents. *Journal of Communication*, 41 (4), 6 – 27.

Erjavec, K. (2001). Media representation of the discrimination against the Roma in Eastern Europe: The case of Slovenia. *Discourse & Society*, 12 (6), 699 – 727.

Fairclough, N. (1988). Discourse representation in media discourse. *Sociolinguistics*, 17: 125 – 139.

Fairclough, N. (1989). *Language and Power*. Harlow: Longman.

Fairclough, N. (1992). *Discourse and Social Change*. Cambridge: Polity Press.

Fairclough, N. (1995). *Media Discourse*. London: Arnold.

Fairclough, N. (1995). *Critical Discourse Analysis*. Boston: Addison Wesley.

Fairclough, N. (2003). *Analysing Discourse: Textual analysis for social research*. London: Routledge.

Ferrarotti, L. (2009). The news presenter and the television audience: a comparative perspective of the use of *we* and *you*. In L. Haarman & L. Lombardo (Eds.), *Evaluation and Stance in War News: A linguistic analysis of American, British and Italian television news reporting of the* 2003 *Iraqi war* (pp. 72 – 96). London: Continuum.

Ferguson, A. (2010). Appraisal in student – supervisor conferencing: a linguistic analysis. *International Journal of Language & Communication Disorders*, 45 (2), 215 – 229.

Fiske, J. (1987). *Television Culture*. London: Methuen.

Fowler R. , Hodge, B. , Kress G. & Trew. , T. (1979). *Language and Control*. London: Routledge.

Fowler, R. (1991). *Language in the News: Discourse and ideology in the press*. London: Routledge.

Gales, T. (2011). Identifying interpersonal stance in threatening discourse: An appraisal analysis. *Discourse Studies*, 13 (1), 27 – 46.

Goffman, E. (1981). *Forms of Talk*. Pennsylvania: University of Pennsylvania Press.

Glasser, T. L. (1992). Objectivity and news bias. In E. D. Cohen (Ed.), *Philosophical Issues in Journalism* (pp. 176 – 185). Oxford: Oxford University Press.

Haarman, L. & Lombardo, L. (2009). *Evaluation and Stance in War News: A linguistic analysis of American, British and Italian television news reporting of the* 2003 *Iraqi war*. New York: Continuum.

Haddington, P. (2004). Stance taking in news interviews. *SKY Journal of Linguistics*, 17: 101 – 142.

Halliday, M. A. (1973). *Explorations in the Functions of Language*. *London: Edward Arnold.*

Halliday, M. A. (1994). *Functional Grammar*. London: Edward Arnold.

Halliday, M. A& Matthiessen, C(1999). *Construing Experience Through Meaning: A language-based approach to cognition.* London: Continuum.

Halliday, M. A& Matthiessen, C(2004). *An Introduction to Functional Grammar* (3rd ed.). London: Edward Arnold.

Hallin, D. C. (1984). The media, the war in Vietnam, and political support: A critique of the thesis of an oppositional media. *The Journal of Politics*, 46 (1), 1 – 24.

Hallin, D. C. (1986). *The Uncensored War: The media and Vietnam*. Oxford: Oxford University Press.

Hartley, J. (1982). *Understanding News*. London: Methuen.

Hartley, J. (1992). *Tele-ology: Studies in television*. London: Routledge.

Hartley, J. (2002). *Communication, Cultural and Media Studies: The key concepts*. London and New York: Routledge.

Hutchby, I. (2011). Non-neutrality and argument in the hybrid political interview. *Discourse Studies*, 13 (3), 349 – 365.

Hunston, S. (2000). Evaluation and the planes of discourse: Status and value in persuasive texts. In S. Hunston & G. Thompson (Eds.), *Evaluation in Text: Authorial stance and the construction of discourse* (pp. 176 – 207). Oxford: Oxford University Press.

Hunston, S. (2011). *Corpus Approaches to Evaluation: Phraseology and evaluative language*. London and New York: Routledge.

Hunston, S. & Thompson, G. (2000). *Evaluation in Text: Authorial stance and the construction of discourse*, Oxford: OUP.

Hyland, K. (2005a). *Metadiscourse: Exploring interaction in writing*. New York: Continuum.

Hyland, K. (2005b). Stance and engagement: a model of interaction in academic discourse. *Discourse Studies*, 7 (2),

173 – 192.

Hyland, K. (2006). Representing readers in writing: Student and expert practices. *Linguistics and Education*, 16 (4), 363 – 377.

Hyland, K. (2007). Applying a gloss: Exemplifying and reformulating in academic discourse. *Applied Linguistics*, 28 (2), 266 – 285.

Hyland, K. (2008). Persuasion, interaction and the construction of knowledge: Representing self and others in research writing. *International Journal of English Studies*, 8 (2), 1 – 23.

Iedema, R., Feez, S & White, P. R. R. (1994). *Media Literacy (Write it Right Literacy in Industry Research Project)* - Stage 2, Sydney: Disadvantaged Schools Program, NSW Department of School Education, with the extracts of chapters are from *http://grammatics. com/appraisal/MediaLit-Appraise. pdf*

IMF. About the IMF. *https://www. imf. org/external/about. htm*

Jaffe, A. (2009). Introduction: the Sociolinguistics of Stance. In A. Jaffe (Ed.), *Stance: Sociolinguistic Perspective* (pp. 3 - 28). Oxford: OUP.

Johnstone, B. (2009). Stance, Style, and the Linguistic Individual. In A. Jaffe (Ed.), *Stance: Sociolinguistic Perspective* (pp. 29 - 52). Oxford: OUP.

Jullian, P. M. (2011). Appraising through someone else's words: The evaluative power of quotations in news reports. *Discourse & Society*, 22 (6), 766 - 780.

Kärkkäinen, E. (2006). Stance taking in conversation: From subjectivity to intersubjectivity. *Text and Talk*, 26 (6), 699 - 731.

Kim, K. H. (2014). Examining U. S. news media discourses about North Korea: A corpus-based critical discourse analysis. *Discourse & Society*, 25 (2), 221 - 244.

Kress, G. & Trew, A. (1978). Ideological transformation of discourse. *Sociological Review*, 26 (4), 755 - 776.

Kress, G. & van Leeuwen, T. (1996). *Reading Images: The grammar of visual design*. London: Routledge.

Kress, G. & van Leeuwen, T. (1998). Front pages: (The critical) analysis of newspaper layout. In A. Bell & P. Garrett (Eds.), *Approaches to Media Discourse* (pp. 186 – 219). Oxford: Blackwell Publishing.

Kroeger, P. (2005). *Analysing Grammar: An Introduction.* Cambridge: Cambridge University Press.

Lee, N. I. (2009). Stance and engagement in writing: Japanese and American editorials. In V. K. Bhatia, W. Cheng, B. Du-Babcock, J. Lung (Eds.) *Language for Professional Communication: Research, practice & training* (pp. 61 – 70). Hong Kong: The Hong Kong Polytechnic University.

Lehman-Wilzig, S. N. & Seletzky, M. (2010). Hard news, soft news, 'general'news: The necessity and utility of an intermediate classification. *Journalism*, 11 (1), 37 – 56.

Liang Y. & Xie, F. (2010). *An Overview of English Language Media of China*, Beijing: Intellectual Property Publishing House.

Liu, Z., (Ed.) (2013). *Chinese Public Opinion Index Report.* Beijing: Social Sciences Academic Press (China) (刘志明编,

2013，中国舆情指数报告，北京：社会科学出版社）.

Lombardo, L. (2009). The news presenter as socio-cultural construct. In L. Haarman & L. Lombardo (Eds.), *Evaluation and Stance in War News: A Linguistic Analysis of American, British and Italian Television News Reporting of the* 2003 *Iraqi War* (pp. 48 – 71). New York: Continuum.

Li, J. (2010). Transitivity and lexical cohesion: Press representations of a political disaster and its actors. *Journal of Pragmatics*, 42 (12), 3444 – 3458.

Luginbuhl, M. (2009). Disclosing and announcing, interpreting and entertaining: A comparative study of the history of TV News presentation. In C. Rowe & E. L. Wyss (Eds.), *Language and New Media: Linguistic, cultural, and technological evolutions* (pp. 245 – 281). Michigan: Hampton Press.

Macken-Horarik, M. (2003). Appraisal and the special instructiveness of narrative. *Text*, 23 (2), 285 – 312.

Macken-Horarik, M. & Isaac, A. (2014). Appraising appraisal. In G. Thompson & L. Alba-Juez (Eds.), *Evaluation in Context* (pp. 242 – 267). Amsterdam: John Benjamins Publishing.

Mancini, P. (1988). Simulated interaction: How the television journalist speaks. *European Journal of Communication*. 3 (2), 151 – 166.

Marin-Arrese, J. I. (1997). Conceptualization of events, transitivity and voice: a cognitive approach. *Cuadernos de Filología Inglesa*, 6 (2), 319 – 332.

Marín-Arrese, J. I., Hidalgo-Downing, L., & Molina-Plaza, S. (2004). Evidential, epistemic and deontic modality in English and Spanish: The expression of writer stance in newspaper discourse. In R. Facchinetti & F. Palmer (Eds.), *English Modality in Perspective: Genre analysis and contrastive studies* (pp. 121 – 139). Frankfurt: Peter Lang.

Martin, J. R. (2000). Beyond exchange: Appraisal systems in English. In S. Hunston, G. Thompson (Eds.), *Evaluation in Text. Authorial stance and the construction of discourse* (pp. 142 – 175). Oxford: OUP.

Martin, J. R. (2004). Mourning: how we get aligned.

Discourse & Society,15 (2 – 3),321 – 344.

Martin,J. R. & White, P. R. R. (2005). *The Language of Evaluation*. New York:Palgrave Macmillan.

Matthiessen, C. & Halliday, M. A. K. (2009). *Systemic Functional Grammar:A first step into the theory*. Beijing:Higher Education Press.

McLuhan, M. (1964). *Understanding Media: Extensions of Man*. New York:McGraw Hill.

McNair, B. (1999). *Journalism and Democracy*. London: Routledge.

Montgomery,M. (2007). *The Discourse of Broadcast News*. New York:Routledge.

Montgomery,M. (2008). The discourse of the broadcast news interview:A typology. *Journalism Studies*, 9 (2),260 – 278.

Montgomery, M. (2011). The accountability interview, politics and change in UK public service broadcasting. In M. Ekstrom & M. Patrona (Eds.), *Talking Politics in the*

Broadcast Media: *Evolving forms of journalism and political accountability* (pp. 33 – 55). Amsterdam: John Benjamins.

O'Keeffe, A. & Breen, M. J. (2007). At the hands of the brothers: a corpus-based lexico-grammatical analysis of stance in newspaper reporting of child sexual abuse cases. In J. Cotterill (Ed.), *The Language of Sexual Crime* (pp. 217 – 236). London: Palgrave Macmillan.

Page, R. E. (2003). An analysis of APPRAISAL in childbirth narratives with special consideration of gender and storytelling style. *Text*, 23 (2), 211 – 238.

Park, R. E. (1940). News as a form of knowledge: A chapter in the sociology of knowledge. *American Journal of Sociology*, 45 (5), 669 – 686.

Partington, A. (2004). Utterly content in each other's company: Semantic prosody and semantic preference. *International Journal of Corpus Linguistics*, 9 (1), 131 – 156.

Pérez-González, L. (2007). Appraising dubbed conversation: Systemic functional insights into the construal of naturalness in translated film dialogue. *The Translator*, 13 (1), 1 – 38.

Piazza, R. (2009). News is reporting what was said: Techniques and patterns of attribution. In L. Haarman & L. Lombardo (Eds.), *Evaluation and Stance in War News: A Linguistic analysis of American, British and Italian television news reporting of the 2003 Iraqi war* (pp. 170 – 195). New York: Continuum.

Pounds, G. (2010). Attitude and subjectivity in Italian and British hard-news reporting: The construction of a culture-specific 'reporter' voice'. *Discourse Studies*, 12 (1), 106 – 137.

Pounds, G. (2012). Multimodal expression of authorial affect in a British television news programme. *Discourse, Context & Media*, 1 (2), 68 – 81.

Radford, A. (2004). *English Syntax: An introduction.* Cambridge: Cambridge University Press.

Reinemann, C. Stanyer, J., Scherr, S. & Legnante, G. (2012). Hard and soft news: A review of concepts, operationalizations and key findings. *Journalism*, 13 (2), 221 – 239.

Rowe, C. & Wyss, E. L. (2009). *Language and New Media: Linguistic, cultural, and technological evolutions.* Michigan:

Hampton Press.

Ryan, M. (2001). Journalistic ethics, objectivity, existential journalism, standpoint epistemology, and public journalism. *Journal of Mass Media Ethics*, 16 (1), 3 – 22.

Sano M (2008). The rhetoric of editorials: A Japanese case study. In: E. Thompson and P. R. R. White (Eds.), *Communicating Conflict: Multilingual case studies of the new media* (pp. 97 – 118). London: Continuum.

Scannell, P. (1998). Media, language, world. In A. Bell & P. Garrett (Eds.), *Approaches to Media Discourse* (pp. 252 – 267). Oxford: Blackwell.

Schiffrin, D. (1986). *Discourse Markers*. Cambridge: CUP.

Schudson, M. (2003). *The Sociology of News*. New York: Norton.

Seo, S. (2013). Hallidayean transitivity analysis: The battle for Tripoli in the contrasting headlines of two national newspapers. *Discourse & Society*. 24 (6), 774 – 791.

Shoemaker, P. J. & Reese, S. D. (1996). *Mediating the Message: Theories of influences on mass media content*. New York: Longman.

Shoemaker, P. J., & Cohen, A. A. (2006). *News Around the World: Content practitioners and the public*. New York: Routledge.

Sinclair, J. (1981). Planes of discourse. In R. Mohan & S. N. A. Rizvi (Eds.), *The two-fold voice: essays in honour of Ramesh Mohan* (pp. 70 – 89). Salzburg: University of Salzburg.

Sinclair, J. (1986). Fictional worlds: Talking about text. In M. Coulthard (Ed.), *Talking about Text* (pp. 43 – 60). University of Birmingham: English Language Research.

Sinclair, J. (1991). *Corpus, Concordance, Collocation*. Oxford: Oxford University Press.

Sinclair, J. (1996). The search for units of meaning. *Textus*, 9 (1), 75 – 106.

Sinclair, J (2003). *Reading Concordances*. London: Pearson Education Limited.

Swan, M. (2005). *Practical English Usage*. Oxford: Oxford University Press.

Stubbs, M. (2001). *Words and Phrases: Corpus studies of lexical semantics*. Oxford: Blackwell Publishers.

Stenvall, M. (2008). On emotions and the journalistic ideals of factuality and objectivity: Tools for analysis. *Journal of Pragmatics*, 40 (9), 1569 – 1586.

Teo, P. (2000). Racism in the news: A critical discourse analysis of news reporting in two Australian newspapers. *Discourse & Society*, 11 (1), 7 – 49.

Thetela, P. (1997). Evaluated entities and parameters of value in academic research articles. *English for Specific Purposes*, 16 (2), 101 – 118.

Thompson, G. (1996). *Introduction to Functional Grammar*. London: Edward Arnold.

Thompson, G. & Alba-Juez, L. (2014). *Evaluation in Context*. Amsterdam: John Benjamins Publishing Company.

Thompson, G. & Hunston, S. (2000). Evaluation: an introduction. In S. Hunston & G. Thompson (Eds.), *Evaluation in Text: Authorial stance and the construction of discourse* (pp. 1 – 27). Oxford: OUP.

Thomson, E. & White, P. R. R. (2008). *Communicating Conflict: Multilingual case studies of the news media*. London: Continuum.

Thomson, E. A., White, P. R. & Kitley, P. (2008). Objectivity and 'hard news' reporting across cultures: Comparing the news report in English, French, Japanese and Indonesian journalism. *Journalism studies*, 9 (2), 212 – 228.

Thornborrow, J. & Montgomery, M. (2010). Special issue on personalization in the broadcast news interview. *Discourse & Communication*, 4 (2), 99 – 104.

Tuchman, G. (1972). Objectivity as strategic ritual: An examination of newsmen's notion of objectivity. *American Journal of Sociology*. 77 (4), 660 – 679.

van Dijk. T. A. (1985). Structure of news in press. In T. A. van Dijk (Ed.), *Discourse and Communication* (pp. 69 – 93).

New York: de Gruyter.

van Dijk, T. A. (1987). *Communicating Racism: Ethnic prejudice in thought and talk*. London: Sage Publications, Inc.

van Dijk. T. A. (1988a). *News as Discourse.* Hillsdale: lawrence Erlbaum.

van Dijk, T. A. (1988b). How 'they' hit the headlines. In G. Smitherman, & T. A. van Dijk (Eds.), *Discourse and Discrimination* (pp. 221 – 263). Detroit: Wayne State University Press.

van Dijk. T. A. (1988c). *News Analysis: Case studies of international & national news in the press*. Hillsdale, NJ: Lawrence Erlbaum.

van Dijk, T. A. (1991). *Racism and the Press*. London: Routledge.

Van Dijk, T. (*A*) (1996). Power and the news media. In (*D*) Paletz (Ed.), *Political Communication and Action* (pp. 9 – 36). Cresskill, NJ: Hampton Press.

van Hout, T., Vertommen, B. & Pounds, G. (2012).

Analysing the view from here, there and nowhere: Discursive approaches to journalistic stance. *Discourse, Context & Media*, 1 (2), 55 – 56.

van Leeuwen, T. (1996). The representation of social actors. In C. R. Caldas-Coulthard & M. Coulthard (Eds.), *Texts and Practices: Readings in critical discourse analysis* (pp. 32 – 70). London: Psychology Press.

Tran, VTH. & Thomson, E. A. (2008). The nature of the 'reporter voice: a Vietnamese hard news story. In E. A. Thomson and P. R. R. White (Eds.), *Communicating Conflict: Multilingual case studies of the news media* (pp. 51 – 64). London: Continuum.

Wang, Z. (2004). An appraisal approach to hard news in both English and Chinese: Appraisal systems inquiry. *Foreign Language Education*, 25 (5), 31 – 35 (王振华. "硬新闻"的态度研究——"评价系统"应用研究之二 [J] 外语教学. 2004. 25 (5), 31 – 35)

Wang, Z., (2001). Appraisal systems and their operation: A new development in the Systemic Functional Linguistics. *Journal of Foreign Languages* 136 (6), 13 – 20 (王振华. 评价系统及其运作[J]. 外国语. 2001. 136 (6), 13 – 20)

White, P. P. R. (1997). Death, disruption and the moral order: Narrative impulse in mass-media 'hard news' reporting. In F. Christie & J. R. Martin (Eds.) *Genre and Institutions: Social processes in the workplace and school* (pp. 101 – 133). London: Cassell.

White, P. R. R. (1998). *Telling Media Tales: the news story as rhetoric*. Unpublished PhD dissertation, Sydney: University of Sydney.

White, P. R. R. (2000). Media objectivity and the rhetoric of news story structure. In E. Ventola (Ed.), *Discourse and Community: Doing functional linguistics* (pp. 379 – 397). Tübingen: Gunter narr Verlag Tübingen.

White, P. R. R. (2003). Beyond modality and hedging: A dialogic view of the language of intersubjective stance. *Text and Talk*, 23 (2), 259 – 284.

White, P. R. R. (2004). Subjectivity, evaluation and point of view in media discourse. In C. Coffin (Ed.), *Applying English Grammar: Functional and corpus approaches* (pp. 229 – 246). London: Arnold.

White, P. R. R (2006). Evaluative semantics and ideological

positioning in journalistic discourse-a new framework for analysis. In I. Lassen, (Ed.), *Mediating Ideology in Text and Image: Ten critical studies* (pp. 37 – 68). Amsterdam: John Benjamins.

White, P. R. (2009). Media power and the rhetorical potential of the ‘hard news’ report – attitudinal mechanisms in journalistic discourse. In *VAKKI Symposium XXIX*, conducted at University of Vaasa, Finland, Vaasa, Finland.

White, P. R. R. (2011). Appraisal. In J. Zienkowski, J. Ostman & J. Verschueren (Eds.), *Handbook of Pragmatics* (pp. 14 –36). Amsterdam: John Benjamins.

White, P. R. R (2012). Exploring the axiological workings of ‘reporter voice’ news stories – Attribution and attitudinal positioning. *Discourse, Context & Media*. (1)2 –3, 57 –67.

White, P. R. R., & Thomson, E. A. (2008). The news story as rhetoric: Linguistic approaches to the analysis of journalistic discourse. In E. Thomson& P. R. R. White (Eds.), *Communicating Conflict: Multilingual case studies of the news media* (pp. 1 –24). New York: Continuum.

Wodak, R. & Fairclough, N. (1997). Critical discourse

analysis. In T. A. van Dijk (Ed.), *Discourse as Social Interaction* (*pp*. 258 –284). London: Sage.

Wodak, R. (2000). Recontextualization and the transformation of meanings: A critical discourse analysis of decision making in EU-meetings about employment policies. In S. Sarangi & M. Coulthard (Eds.), *Discourse and Social Life* (pp. 185 –206). Harlow: Pearson Education.

Wodak, R., & Matouschek, B. (1993). We are dealing with people whose origins one can clearly tell just by 'looking': Critical discourse analysis and the study of neo-racism in contemporary Austria. *Discourse & Society*, 4 (2), 225 –248.

Zappavigna, M. (2011). Ambient affiliation: A linguistic perspective on Twitter. *New Media & Society*, 13 (5), 788 –806.

Zappavigna, M. (2012). *Discourse of Twitter and Social Media: How we use language to create affiliation on the web.* New York: Continuum.

Appendices

Appendix 1

The Professional Ethics of Chinese Journalism

(Main items translated by the author from Chinese to English)

(Amended on November 9,2009,The Seventh Council of the All-China Journalists Association,the second plenary session)

1. To serve the people wholeheartedly. Journalists should be loyal to the party and loyal to the motherland, to the people; should seek the unity of embodiment of the party's views and reflection of people's wishes and seek the unity of adherence to the correct orientation and accessibility society and public opinion and seek the unity of adherence to positive propaganda and strengthening its role of public supervision; should play the role of party and the government being as a link with the people.

2. To insist on correct guidance of public opinion. Journalists should adhere to the unity and stability and encourage positive propaganda and sing the main theme, and

constantly consolidate and strengthen the positive and healthy public opinion.

3. To adhere to the principles of truth of the news. Journalists should regard truth as the life of news and should adhere to the thorough investigation and study in order to report the truth accurately, comprehensively and objectively.

4. To carry forward the fine style. Journalists should establish a correct outlook on the world, life and values to strengthen the moral character and improve the overall quality and to resist unhealthy tendency and accept social supervision.

5. To persist in reform and innovation. Journalists should follow the law of journalism and communication to improve the ability of guiding public opinions and to generate innovative ideas, innovative content, innovative forms, innovative methods, innovative means so as to conform to the times and the law of the journalism and to be creative in practice.

6. Be Compliant. Journalists should enhance the concept of abiding to the law: to abide by the Constitution, the laws and the regulations and to comply with the party's discipline in journalism, thus, safeguarding national interests and security and keeping state secrets.

7. To promote the exchange and cooperation of the international news counterparts. Journalists should strive to

cultivate a vision of the world and international perspective and actively build a bridge of communication between China and the world.

Appendix 2

Selected Data

Sample 1: *BBC World News* (20 news items)

Date	Item Number	Case 1: Syria crisis
01-09-2012	1.	United Nation's children's agency says [attribute, acknowledge] the crisis in Syria could be one of the biggest humanitarian emergencies [appreciation,-valuation] of the last few decades. The warning [affect,-security] [attribute, distance] comes as Syrian refugees complain of [affect,-happiness] *poor* [appreciation,-composition] conditions on the border with Turkey. More than two hundred thousand Syrians have now fled their country.
02-09-2012	2.	The *new* [judgement, + normality] UN envoy to Syria, Lakhdar Brahimi, says [attribute, acknowledge] Syrian government must respond to the legitimate [judgement, + tenacity] demands of its people. On Mr. Brahimi's first official day in his post, Syrian government announced [attribute, acknowledge] that forces loyal [judgement, + veracity] to president Assad has repelled a large scale attack [judgement,-propriety] by rebels on an air force college near the city of Aleppo. Meanwhile, Jordon has issued a joint call with the UN's refugee agency for seven-hundred million dollars in order to help [judgement, + propriety] care for the *growing* [appreciation,-reaction] number of refugees from the fighting [judgement,-propriety] in Syria. More than a hundred and eighty thousand [graduation,-force, quantification] Syrians are currently *in shelter* [affect,-happiness] in Jordon, many of them at *specially constructed* [appreciation, + reaction] *camps*. A little earlier I asked UN Higher Commission for Refugees spokesperson in Jordon, Andrew Harper, whether the number of Syrian refugees had taken his organization by surprise [affect,-security].

(续上表)

Date	Item Number	Case 1: Syria crisis
02 – 09 – 2012	3.	The Jordanian government has *nearly doubled* [judgement, + capacity] its estimates of the amount of money. It *needs* [judgement, + propriety] to cope with [judgement, + propriety] the influx of refugees [appreciation, -reaction] from Syria. In an appeal issued jointly with the United Nations, Jordan says [attribute, acknowledge] it *urgently needs* [irrelis affect, + inclination] seven-hundred million dollars. More than a hundred and eighty thousand Syrians [graduation, -force, quantification] are *currently sheltering* [affect, -happiness] in Jordan. The country is struggling [affect, -security] to meet their needs. Gale Gavlick reports from Amman.
03 – 09 – 2012	4.	The *new* [judgement, + normality] International UN envoy to Syria Lahdar Brahimi has described the task ahead of him as *'nearly impossible'* [appreciation, -valuation] who's speaking to the BBC's Lyse Doucet after taking up a *new* [judgement, + normality] job. Mr. Brahimi admitted being scared of [realis affect, -security] *the weight of responsibility* [appreciation, + composition] he is carrying. He acknowledged [attribute, acknowledge] that the international community was doing little to stop people in Syria dying [neg. + judgement, + propriety].

Date	Item Number	Case 2: Eurozone Crisis
09 – 10 – 2012	5.	Hello and welcome. The International Monetary Fund says [attribute, acknowledge] there have been *new* [appreciation, -reaction] setbacks [appreciation, -valuation] in attempts [affect, + inclination] to nurse [judgement, + tenacity] the world economy back to recovery. The IMF has now *lowered its forecast* [judgement, -normality] for global growth to just over 3% for this year and next. It says [attribute, acknowledge]. the *main* [appreciation, -reaction] problem [appreciation, -reaction] is that economic

（续上表）

Date	Item Number	Case 2: Eurozone Crisis
		policy in developing economies has failed to rebuild confidence [judgement,-capacity]. It also says [attribute,acknowledge] that investors are most worried about [affect,-security] the viability of the Euro zone and the state of the U. S. government's finances. James Kelly has more.
09 – 10 – 2012	6.	She's [Merkel] making her first visit to Greece for the first time since the debt crisis erupted. This visit is intended [affect, + inclination] to show support [judgement, + tenacity] for the Greek government as it attempts to [judgement, + normality] push through the tough [appreciation,-reaction] austerity measures to cut its deficit. On the eve of this, though, thousands of demonstrators [affect,-satisfaction] have been on the streets. They've been *chanting anti-austerity slogans* [affect,-happiness] and warning [affect,-security] [attribute, distance] Angela Merkel that she's not *welcome* [neg. affect, + happiness] in their country. From Athens, Mark Lowen has more.
09 – 10 – 2012	7.	It's midday here in London, seven a. m. in Washington, and two in the afternoon in the Greek capital Athens, where Angela Merkel has just arrived for her first visit in five years. What a five years it has been [affect,-satisfaction]. The Greece she'll see this time around is mired in recession [appreciation,-composition] and its people angry about [affect,-happiness] the austerity package that has followed. Much of that anger [affect,-happiness] is actually directed at the German leader herself and some of it is quite nasty [appreciation,-reaction; affect,-happiness] too. So why is Angela Merkel flying into the flack [judgement,-propriety]. Here's our Athens correspondent Mark Lowen.

(续上表)

Date	Item Number	Case 2: Eurozone Crisis
10-10-2012	8.	Hello and welcome. The IMF is in Tokyo for its annual meeting. Top of the agenda is how to get the global economy growing more rapidly [judgement, + capacity]. It's warned [affect,-security] [attribute, distance] that the risks [appreciation,-reaction] to financial stability worldwide have risen in the past six months, and despite efforts to resolve [judgement, + tenacity] the Eurozone debt crisis the region is still seen as the main risk [appreciation,-composition] to global financial stability. The director of the IMF's monetary capital markets Jose Vinals has been speaking in the past few hours. He outlined what the IMF believes [affect, + inclination] *must* [judgement, + propriety] be done in the Eurozone.
Date	**Item Number**	**Case 3: Boston Bombing**
16-04-2013	9.	Welcome back. The FBI has taken over the investigation [judgement, + veracity] into the two *explosions* [judgement,-propriety] in the Boston Marathon which left three people dead [judgement,-propriety] and at least a hundred forty others injured [judgement,-propriety]. Police have said [attribute, acknowledge] to be *working around the clock* [judgement, + tenacity] and *all leave has been cancelled* [judgement, + tenacity]. The news continues to *make waves* [appreciation, + reaction] overseas with many world leaders extending their sympathies [affect,-happiness] to the victims and their loved ones. British Prime Minister David Cameron released a statement saying [attribute, acknowledge] the scenes from Boston are shocking [affect,-security]. That's a quote from him. "*My thoughts,*" he says [attribute, acknowledge], "*are with all those who have been affected* [affect,-happiness]." Julia Gillard, the Australian prime minister said [attribute, acknowledge] our condolences [affect,-happiness] go to the families of those *killed* [judgement,-propriety]. These explosions have cast a long shadow over [affect,-security] one of the world's great sporting events [appreciation, + valuation]." And the president of Afganistan Hamid Karzai sent his condolences [affect,-

（续上表）

Date	Item Number	Case 3: Boston Bombing
		happiness] arising from *such incidents* [judgement,-propriety]. "Well, with me is Emily Buchanan for more the international reaction to this event. Emily—
16-04-2013	10.	It's midday here in London, and seven in the morning in Boston, a city that should be celebrating [affect, + happiness] the end of its annual Marathon but instead *dealing with* [affect,-happiness] the aftermath [appreciation,-reaction] of the worst bombing [appreciation,-reaction] on U. S. soil since 9/11. Three people [graduation,-force, quantification] were *killed* [judgement,-propriety] and a hundred and forty spectators and competitors [graduation,-force, quantification] were *injured* [judgement,-propriety]. President Obama has said [attribute, acknowledge] that those responsible [judgement,-propriety] for these acts will feel the full weight justice [judgement, + propriety]. Let's go over to Boston now. We are joined by the BBC's Laura Travelyn.
17-04-2013	11.	We have learned from the White House the president will be going up to Boston for what's been called *an interfaith service* [appreciation, + valuation] on Thursday in memorial of [judgement, + propriety] those who were attacked [judgement,-propriety] at the Marathon. We've also heard from the FBI that they have recovered what they think are fragments of a black nylon bag that was used to hold the bomb [appreciation,-reaction]. The bomb [appreciation,-reaction] we were told contained nails, ball bearings [appreciation,-composition] and was possibly inside a pressure cooker. But the FBI's saying [attribute, acknowledge] that the range of suspects and motives is *still wide* [affect,-security]. I am Katty Kay, thanks so much for watching and do stay here for more on world news America.

（续上表）

Date	Item Number	Case 3: Boston Bombing
17－04－2013	12.	Welcome to our viewers on public television in America and also around the globe. "We will *go to the ends of earth* [judgement, + tenacity] to identify those *responsible* [judgement,-propriety] for this *unspeakable* [affect,-happiness] crime [judgement,-propriety]." That was the promise [affect, + inclination] today from the FBI agent in charge of the investigation into the Boston bombings. But a day later, we still don't know who carried out these attacks [judgement,-propriety] or why. The White House has just announced [attribute, acknowledge] the president Obama will travel to Boston for *an interfaith service* [appreciation, + valuation] on Thursday. The BBC's Laura Trevelyan is on the scene. She joins us now in a city, Laura, I imagine still quite in shock [affect,-security].

Date	Item Number	Case 4: Typhoon Haiyan in the Philippines
08－11－2013	13.	Hello, everyone, millions of people in the Philippines have fled from the part one of the strongest [appreciation,-reaction] Typhoon ever to make a landfall with the wind more than three hundred kilometers an hour [appreciation,-composition]. Typhoon Haiyan is a category five super [appreciation,-composition] storm with torrential rain and waves of up to six meters high. It has brought severe [appreciation,-reaction] flooding. Three people [graduation,-force, quantification] are so far known to have *died* [judgement,-normality]. The BBC's Nick Childs has this update.
11－11－2013	14.	'Absolute bedlam' [appreciation,-reaction] that's how the head of Red Cross's described the situation in the Philippines. Four million people [graduation,-force, quantification] have been affected [judgement,-normality] by Typhoon Haiyan, many people are struggling [judgement,-capacity] to survive now without food, shelter or clean drinking water, a huge international relief effort [judgement, + propriety] is under way, but real challenges [appreciation,-composition] including bad [appreciation,-reaction]

(续上表)

Date	Item Number	Case 4: Typhoon Haiyan in the Philippines
		'Absolute bedlam' [appreciation,-reaction] that's how the head of Red Cross's described the situation in the Philippines. Four million people [graduation,-force, quantification] have been affected [judgement,-normality] by Typhoon Haiyan, many people are struggling [judgement,-capacity] to survive now without food, shelter or clean drinking water, a huge international relief effort [judgement, + propriety] is under way, but real challenges [appreciation,-composition] including bad [appreciation,-reaction]
12-11-2013	15.	Hello and welcome, nearly five days after a devastating [appreciation,-composition] typhoon ripped through [appreciation,-reaction] the central Philippines, the scale of the task facing aid agencies is becoming apparent [judgement, + tenacity]. The United Nations has raised its estimate of those affected [judgement,-normality] to more than eleven million people [graduation,-force, quantification]. There's no clear figure yet for the number of people who might have died [judgement,-normality], but the UN humanitarian chief has told the BBC world news many places look *as though they have experienced tsunami but huge boats washed inland in the towns and villages* [appreciation,-reaction]. The United Nations is now appealing for [affect, + inclination] more than MYM300 million. The U. S. is sending an aircraft carrier and several other ships. But in the Philippines itself, rescue workers are still struggling [judgement,-capacity] to reach many areas cut off by the storm [appreciation,-reaction]. The BBC's Tim Willcox reports from the island of Cebu which has become a logistics hub for the UN aid operation.

（续上表）

Date	Item Number	Case 4：Typhoon Haiyan in the Philippines
13 – 11 – 2013	16.	Hello and welcome, the Philippine government has said [attribute, acknowledge] that it is confronting its greatest logistical challenge [appreciation, -composition] ever and has admitted it is overwhelmed [appreciation, -reaction]. Aid supplies [judgement, + propriety] are beginning to reach some of those affected [judgement, + capacity] but it's not easy, because Typhoon Haiyan affected [appreciation, -reaction] the vast area cutting off roads, electricity supplies and communications. In some places there has been no sign of any help coming [judgement, -propriety], in our first report, Alastair Leithead has been trying to reach [judgement, + capacity] isolated [appreciation, + reaction] communities, he took a boat from a remote [appreciation, -reaction] part of Cebu to the western coast of Leyte island and met two sisters heading off on a rescue mission [judgement, + propriety].

Sample 2：*CCTV News Update* (20 news items)

Date	Item Number	Case 1：Syria crisis
02 – 09 – 2012	1.	Jordan is beginning to feel the pressure [affect, -security] of *a mounting influx of Syrian refugees* [appreciation, -reaction] into the country. It has appealed for [affect, + inclination] international community's assistance [judgement, + propriety] to cope with [judgement, + capacity] the situation. Kino has this story
02 – 09 – 2012	2.	The *new* [judgement, + normality] UN envoy to Syria says [attribute, acknowledge] President Bashar Assad's government *should realize* [judgement, + propriety] that the need [affect, + inclination] for change is both "urgent" and "necessary" [appreciation, + valuation]. Lakhdar Brahimi [made the remarks on Saturday in an interview with al-Arabiya television].

（续上表）

Date	Item Number	Case 1: Syria crisis
03-09-2012	3.	Two Syrian activist groups have said [attribute, acknowledge] about 5,000 people [graduation, -force, quantification] were *killed* [judgement, -propriety] in Syria last month, making it the deadliest month [appreciation, -reaction] since the revolt [judgement, -propriety] against President Bashar al-Assad began. According to [attribute, acknowledge] {the British-based Syrian Observatory for Human Rights and The Local Coordination Committees, more than 4,000 of those *killed* [judgement, -propriety] were civilians}.
06-09-2012	4.	First of all, let's go to Syria where violence [appreciation, -reaction] continues across the country. The Syrian Observatory for Human Rights says [attribute, acknowledge] more than 100 *Syrians* [graduation, -force, quantification] were *killed* [judgement, -propriety] on Wednesday, including 76 *unarmed civilians* [judgement, -propriety], 11 *activist fighters* [judgement, -propriety], 3 *defected soldiers* [judgement, -propriety], and 12 *members of the Syrian regular forces* [judgement, -propriety]. EM Kino has the details.

Date	Item Number	Case 2: Eurozone Crisis
02-10-2012	5.	Unemployment [judgement, -normality] in the 17-nation Eurozone remained at its record *high* [appreciation, -reaction] rate of 11.4 percent in August. The *new* [appreciation, + reaction] data has renewed concerns [affect, -security] that measures to slash debt have *sacrificed* [appreciation, -reaction] jobs. The unemployment rate which is the *highest* [appreciation, -reaction] since the euro was created in 1999 -is the same as July's, which was revised up from 11.3on Monday.

（续上表）

Date	Item Number	Case 2：Eurozone Crisis
04 – 10 – 2012	6.	[It's very interesting to (unaudible) time, let's head to watch Europe] figures released earlier in the day shows [attribute, acknowledge] the Eurozone economy has contracted [appreciation, -composition] further at the end of the third quarter this year. Both business activity and new orders in the Eurozone's services sector *continues to fall* [appreciation, -reaction], leading to mounting job losses [judgement, -normality].
05 – 10 – 2012	7.	Let's move on to Europe now where The ECB (European Central Bank) has announced [attribute, acknowledge] it will keep its main interest rate *unchanged* [judgement, + tenacity] at a record *low of* 0.75 *per cent* [appreciation, - reaction]. The Governing Council of the ECB also decided [attribute, acknowledge] that the interest rates on the marginal lending facility and the deposit facility will remain *unchanged* [judgement, + tenacity] at 1.5 percent and 0 percent respectively.
18 – 10 – 2012	8.	European Union countries are considering [affect, + inclination] creating a body inside the European Central Bank. The purpose is to find a legally watertight [appreciation, + valuation] way to involve states outside the Eurozone in a banking union. On Thursday, European leaders will try [affect, + inclination] to bridge divisions over [judgement, + tenacity] a banking union intended [affect, + inclination] to *underpin* [judgement, + tenacity] the Eurozone. They will address how to cater for the 10 EU countries that do not use the euro. Officials from the 27 EU member states have already examined ways to give non-Eurozone countries that join the scheme a say in *supervisory* decisions [appreciation, + composition]. The Financial Times reports that a legal [appreciation, + valuation] opinion prepared for finance

(续上表)

Date	Item Number	Case 2: Eurozone Crisis
		ministers says [attribute, acknowledge] the plan to create a single Eurozone banking supervisor is illegal [judgement, -propriety]. It says [attribute, acknowledge] EU law *does not permit* [neg. + judgement, + propriety] such changes [affect, -security] in how the ECB works.
16 – 04 – 2013	9.	So in our update now, two people [graduation, -force, quantification] have *died* [judgement, -propriety] in Boston and four (um) twenty at least twenty eight [graduation, -force, quantification] have been *injured* [judgement, -propriety] in the U. S. after a pair of explosive devices went off near the finish line of the Boston Marathon tragedy [appreciation, -valuation]. There has been a *loud* [appreciation, -reaction] explosion on the north side of Boylston Street, which is about an hour or so after the winners had crossed the line. Another *thunderous* [appreciation, -reaction] explosion immediately followed (um) after a few seconds. Now Six of the *injured* [judgement, -propriety] are in now *critical* [appreciation, -reaction] condition. Intelligence officials say [attribute, acknowledge] at least one more explosive device was found. In the meantime, over Washington, U. S. President Barack Obama has directed his administration to provide whatever assistance [judgement, + propriety] that is *necessary* [appreciation, + valuation]. Also in the meantime, The U. S. federal source says [attribute, acknowledge] this was a "well-planned" [appreciation, -composition] event. The Boston police commission is now holding a news conference on these twin *explosions* [appreciation, -reaction] and we'll keep you updated as more information develops.

（续上表）

Date	Item Number	Case 3：Boston Bombing
17 – 04 – 2013	10.	Of the over 180 people being treated at hospitals, at least 17 are in critical [appreciation, -reaction] condition (and) 41 are in serious [appreciation, -reaction] condition. As of Tuesday afternoon, at least 51 have gone home. Hospital officials say [attribute, acknowledge] many victims *suffered injuries* [appreciation, -reaction] to the lower parts of their bodies. Boston Tufts Medical Center has cared for 14 victims, and all of them have shrapnel from the blasts [appreciation, -valuation].
17 – 04 – 2013	11.	The Boston Marathon bombings have *rocked* [affect, -security] the United States and *alarmed* [affect, -security] the world. Cities around the globe are taking a closer look [judgement, + normality] at security precautions [judgement, + tenacity] before major events. British officials {have confirmed they're making security their greatest concern [judgement, + tenacity] at the upcoming funeral of former Prime Minister, Margaret Thatcher}.
17 – 04 – 2013	12.	In response to the Boston Marathon bombing, U. S. President Barack Obama has hailed the police response [judgement, + tenacity] and said [attribute, acknowledge] it was *still unknown* [appreciation, -reaction] who was *responsible* [judgement, -propriety]. Speaking on Tuesday from the White House, he described the blasts [appreciation, -valuation] as an "act of terror" [appreciation, -valuation].
Date	Item Number	Case 4：Typhoon Haiyan in the Philippines
10 – 11 – 2013	13.	Philippine President Benigno Aquino III has warned [affect, -security] [attribute, distance] that the *death toll* [appreciation, -composition] from the *super* [appreciation, -reaction] typhoon Haiyan will rise. But he adds that the government will be able to [judgement, + capacity] meet people's basic needs [judgement, + propriety]. He {has also vowed to handle [judgement, +

（续上表）

Date	Item Number	Case 4: Typhoon Haiyan in the Philippines
		tenacity] the aftermath [appreciation,-reaction] of the typhoon, saying [attribute, acknowledge] it would be a tragedy [appreciation,-valuation] if that were mismanaged [judgement,-capacity]. }
10 – 11 – 2013	14.	Despite an official [appreciation,-valuation] *death toll* of 229 [appreciation,-composition], authorities in the Philippines fear [affect,-security] that *super* [appreciation,-reaction] typhoon Haiyan may have *killed* [judgement,-normality] over 10, 000 people [graduation,-force, quantification] in the central province of Leyte alone. A regional police chief has been quoted as saying [attribute, acknowledge] the storm destroyed [appreciation,-composition] 70 to 80 percent of structures in its path. Quentin Vigne has more details.
11 – 11 – 2013	15.	Of course worst-hit [affect,-happiness] was in the Philippines, Officials now say [attribute, acknowledge] the death toll [appreciation,-composition] from *super* [appreciation,-reaction] Typhoon Haiyan could top 10, 000 [graduation,-force, quantification] as entire towns have been completely wiped out [appreciation,-reaction]. Our correspondent Barnaby Lo was at one of the scenes of devastation [appreciation,-composition] and he filed what's now being in record, eyewitness report.
12 – 11 – 2013	16.	Three days after *super* [appreciation,-reaction] typhoon Haiyan made landfall in the Philippines as the full extent of the damage at ground zero [appreciation,-reaction] is now becoming apparent, rescue work *ploughs on* [judgement, + propriety] in most disaster-hit [appreciation,-composition] areas. And international aid [judgement, +propriety] is pouring into the country for disaster relief [judgement, + propriety]. Jiaoyang has more.